The Alignment Effect

The Missing Link Between Where You Are and Where You Want to Be

---

Tyler Watson

The Alignment Effect
Copyright © 2021 by (Tyler Watson)

All rights reserved. No part of this book may be reproduced or transmitted in any form or by any means without written permission from the author.

"Abundance Alignment Technique" and "Abundance Alignment" are registered trademarks of Freedom Catalyst LLC. All rights reserved

ISBN

Table Of Contents

Foreword by Dana Derricks.. 5

Preface 9

Introduction 13

SECTION 1: HOW TO FIND THE "HIDDEN 98%" OF YOUR PERSONAL POWER...AND WHY MOST PERSONAL DEVELOPMENT PROCESSES ARE INCOMPLETE OR DEAD WRONG

Chapter 1: "The Discovery That Changed My Life... And Allowed My Wife to Eat Pizza Again"..19

Chapter 2: "Everything I Thought I Knew About Personal Development Was Wrong...and Here's Why" 29

Chapter 3: "My Leaky House Revealed My Struggles in Business... And How Einstein Really Did Have All The Answers!"....................39

Chapter 4: "It's NOT 'All in Your Mind,' and How Chicken Nuggets and Green Peppers Prove It...The Truth That Lives Beyond Mindset"... 47

Chapter 5: "The ONE Thing to Understand if You Want Results Fast... and What Puke Has To Do With 10xing My Income"........53

Chapter 6: "Why The Supercomputer in Your Body Doesn't Know What You Really Want (It's Not What You Think...Literally!)"....59

Chapter 7: "Why 95% of your problems can actually be changed...and the other 5% can too"..71

SECTION TWO: THE SECRET PROCESSES THE GURUS DIDN'T WANT YOU TO KNOW

Chapter 8: "The Unstoppable Success Equation...How to Get Anything You Want"...79

Chapter 9: "If You Want Success, DON'T Do This! The Plague of Personal Development, Outsourcing, and Waiting" 87

Chapter 10: "What to do Every Week if You Want Success...and How My Daughter's Fear of the Dark Can Get You There" 97

Chapter 11: "The Ten Things You Need to Know to Move at Lightning Speed...and What The Doctors Couldn't Believe" 107

Chapter 12: "Step-by-step Instructions On How to Program Every Cell in Your Body and Get Your Goals in Days Instead of Years" 113

SECTION 3: TAKING IT TO THE NEXT LEVEL AND CREATING TRANSFORMATION THAT LASTS

Chapter 13: "Every Part of You Will Resist... Change This and You Will Always Thrive" 123

Chapter 14: "She Couldn't Take a Shower Or Go To Restaurants Until She Did This...And The Choices You Could Make Right Now to Make or Break Your Own Records" 129

Chapter 15: "Three Things That Will Tell You Everything You Need to Know About Yourself" 133

Chapter 16: "The Secret Sauce That Allows You to Collapse Time... And What to do Next" 137

Foreword

"mis·a·ligned
/ˌmisəˈlīnd/
adjective
having an incorrect position or alignment."

Never forget that word.

That word is about to change your life, like it did for me.
You see, as a fellow high-achiever, I find myself being
pinballed between two feelings…

First, I feel like I've accomplished a whole lot more than most and am grateful.

Second, I feel like I've accomplished a whole lot more than most but am not satisfied.

Ever feel that way?

Well, what took me half a lifetime to figure out is what you're about to discover in this book.

First, let me make an analogy for what you're about to experience.

In anything you do, it's very important to have things in alignment.

Your spine, pelvis, hips, etc. should all be aligned for you to walk, run, sit, stand without pain, right?

Your child's bicycle sprockets should be aligned for the chain to be able to properly rotate without falling off, right?

Your vehicle's tires should be aligned for your vehicle to turn smoothly and not wear out your tires, right?

Well, there's something happening in your body, right now, that's the equivalent of any of those examples.

Just like the front tires of your vehicle, there's an important alignment between your mind and body that's likely out of whack.

I thank God for having met Tyler, and for his not just discovering this, but for also sharing it with me (and now, you).

I'll spare you the gory details of exactly what I've been able to do with his help and guidance, but will let you know that I've experienced exactly what you're experiencing.

You know you're destined for more and are headed toward whom you were meant to be, but still find things that get in the way no matter what you do.

Right?

Here's a secret: you're not aligned.

You can (and have) achieve a LOT, even misaligned.

However, once you master Tyler's system for alignment, you'll be overwhelmed with what's possible for you.

Goals will happen in days instead of years.
Goals will go from a "hope" to an expectation.

I know this all sounds a bit crazy right now, but trust me on this. When I first was introduced to this concept, I'll be utterly honest and tell you I thought it was really weird. At first, I thought Tyler was weird. I thought his technique was weird.

...and then I saw the result.

You'll see many examples and stories throughout this book as to what's possible.

The most important thing you can do is read every word, every page, and follow Tyler's lead.

There's something amazing waiting for you on the other side. See you there.

Dana Derricks is an award-winning business owner and is the retainer of a portfolio of world-class services, software, books, and more on marketing for business owners. You can find more, here: www.DanaDerricks.com

Preface

The reason I've written this book is because I know personal change is possible on a deep fundamental level, and that it doesn't have to take months or years to happen. I've seen people struggle far too long for no real reason or accept defeat in one or more areas of their lives even as they succeed in another. This goes for all levels of business, from the high-achieving multimillionaire to the start-up entrepreneur. It also applies to parents, athletes, religious and civic leaders, as well as to children figuring out who they are, or trying to make friends at school.

I want everyone to know that they can change for real. I want to enable them to demystify why they do what they do and help them become the person they know deep inside they are capable of becoming, without getting bogged down by the esoteric, untouchable, and overly complicated stuff that is so often taught as "personal development" today.

For too many years, people have spiraled in circles, struggled unnecessarily with things that they feel are impossible to change, and have just accepted that certain things have to be a certain way. It is time to put an end to endless cyclical patterns, taking too long to attain goals, and/or sacrificing the things that matter most, and step into a new way of living life. This new way of living life encourages and enables you to create your own ideal reality as quickly as possible, with the least amount of struggle.

Using these methods, I've created millions of dollars, have an amazing lifestyle with my wife and my three kids while balancing my health and thriving in virtually all areas of my life. I feel that I'm on this planet to create and make seemingly complex ideas simple. I feel richly blessed and honored to be able to share this wisdom with you, to hopefully help you move beyond the areas in your life that you may have become resigned to, or just believe that they can't be changed. You may have thought "It's just the way it is." If you genuinely want to create massive momentum in your life, triumph in the area that you've settled on and attain your goals in days, instead of years, you should definitely read this book and take action.

These principles have been tried by thousands of people from all backgrounds and walks of life. They have used them in healing and wellness goals, finances and business growth, relationships and family life, and more. You will hear some of their stories in this book, and can find hundreds more online at: Alignmenteffectbook.com

I'm my own continuing "case study" that this works. I came from a disrupted family life and started my working years as a broke massage therapist making less than $15 per session. I undercharged, overworked, and always felt like there was no way to get lasting success in anything. Anytime I got momentum, I would suffer in another part of my life.

At one time, my results were so bad that I remember asking my girlfriend (who later, miraculously, became my wife),

"What would you say to someone who only had 49 cents in their bank account, but wants to make money?"

That 'someone' was me.

Her response was the beginning of a transformation that challenged not only what my mind believed, but what was ingrained into every cell in my BODY. Even though I hated them, the results I was experiencing at that time felt "natural" because every organ, gland, and energy pattern in me was working to keep them that way. Once this shifted through the concepts we will be discussing in this book, I made my first six figures in just a few months.

If you think that "quantum leaps" from one level of life to the next rarely happen, then through this book, you will learn to increase their frequency, know why those special occurrences occur, how to duplicate them, and how to get things working for you instead of against you. If you feel like you have a deeper purpose inside of you that you haven't fully unlocked or tapped into, or you've had massive success in the past but feel like you can't quite get to that next level without repeating some of the same struggles, trust me, you are going to want to keep reading. If you're looking to tap into a deeper power, become unstoppable, create positive self-actualized feeling inside of you, be in control and confident pushing yourself more, and feel powerful and transformed in a lasting way, then you're in the right place.

I thank you for finding this book and know that you're here for a reason. By the time you're done, if you apply the principles in this book, you will experience something phenomenal.

Disclaimer: Align, Aligning, Abundance Alignment concept, the Abundance Alignment Technique and anything found within this book is not intended to diagnose, treat, cure, or prevent any disease, injury, or physical or mental condition. The techniques, skills, practices, et cetera, outlined are informational in nature only. And nothing in this book or any of the training is intended to provide medical advice, nor is it to be used as a substitute for diagnostic action or medical treatment by a qualified, licensed healthcare practitioner. Results are affected by numerous factors and may vary. There are no guarantees or warranties expressed or implied as to any results or effects of the use of this knowledge or techniques. Use of the Abundance Alignment Technique, and/or any material herein or any of its elements constitutes acknowledgement and acceptance of these and any other limitations.

Introduction:

This book was written for those who understand the power of the mind and the body, and who are creators and leaders, entrepreneurs, high-achievers, go-getters, and parents. It is intended to disrupt the mindset industry that is overly focused on repetition, root-causes, and trauma; and instead actually help you create the life you really want in a fraction of the time you've spent working on your "mindset."

As you read, you will come to know that you can truly change within a matter of minutes in a way that lasts and happens on a physical level, not just in the brain. Lasting, powerful change is not a mystery. You have the power to change anything in any area of your life in days, not years. And if you've accepted defeat or become resigned to your "fate", or accepted something as "fact", even though you don't want to; take hope, it doesn't have to be that way. Changing a pattern or a way of life or a symptom that has been going on for years doesn't have to take hundreds of thousands of dollars or thousands of hours.

By the time you are done with this book, you will understand that the fastest way to make a change, whether in finances, in relationships, or in health is not just to change the MIND, but to change the BODY. I've put this to the test after years of struggling, which I'll tell you more about throughout this book.

For instance, a few years ago, I decided to go through some intensive work that was focused primarily on the mind. I wanted to be more productive, organized, and powerful. I wanted to grow my business and relationships. And I ended up spending over $80,000 and a full year putting in almost seven hours a day, five days a week to try to change.

I was dedicated.

I wanted to transform for reals.

Through that experience, I learned a lot. I gained a lot of perspective.

I have also been through techniques like firewalking, arrow breaking, getting to root causes, hypnosis, therapy, visualization, breakthrough experiences, meditation, rituals from tribal cultures, and hundreds of hours of other processes from dozens of very skilled practitioners.

However, the problem with almost all the techniques is that they take too long or were ineffective. You had to do them over and over and over. And if the passion wasn't there, then they didn't work.

I was on a mission to figure out what is the fastest way to make a change and have it last.

That's why I wrote this book.

I discovered something, a paradigm shift and technique that allows me to create and accomplish what used to take me months in just 90 minutes.

And if that sounds too good to be true, keep reading. I'm going to show you proof.

If you're reading this book, you might be thinking, "Tyler just wants me to read this book so I'm willing to go to the next level and learn his full technique?"

If so, the answer is yes! Absolutely. I've seen WAY too many lives changed for good by this to want anything else for you.

However, you don't have to wait to learn the full process to start getting the benefits. In fact, you will take the first steps in the book itself. My goal by the time you're done is for you to have a book that is marked up, underlined, and dog-eared. I want it to be something that you can use as a standalone, apply the principles, use the skills and put it to the test yourself to see and experience your own transformation.

And for those for whom this resonates, or who are looking for a long-term mastery, I have several different, more advanced ways that you can learn the full process, which is broken down into video courses with group coaching and is FAR more extensive than what I can put into this book.

But either way, regardless of what you choose, in order to get the most out of this book, I invite you to (momentarily) set aside your past knowledge or education in this area. What we share here almost certainly will fly in the face of what you think you know about human capacity and transformation. We are going to cover things that will probably make you excited and thinking bigger than ever before. But, they might also make you uncomfortable as you challenge your own assumptions and start confronting everything in your life with new eyes.

So, I invite you to open your mind to a new way of thinking and open your body (which we'll get into more later) into interpreting things on a new level. I invite you to consider things that you may have not have ever thought possible.

And as you do that, you will experience new insights, and get rid of symptoms that no longer serve you. You will see how to increase your income and create better relationships with your spouse or loved ones. Whatever your current focus, I want to help you attain that focus or desired outcome in a fraction of the time that you think it will take.

I truly believe I was put on this earth to simplify and speed up how fast people can change so they can use this earth life as a time to make massive impact and transformations. I'm here to share truth and debunk all the myths and complications so you can find the simplest path possible to lasting change.

I hope that as you're reading this book and implementing all that's inside, it will give you the knowledge and power to transform any area of your life, to never be a victim of your circumstances, to challenge the current way of life, to be better, to be more effective and consistent.

As you implement these tools, techniques, and processes, buckle up and get ready for the ride of your life.

Let's do this.

SECTION 1: HOW TO FIND THE "HIDDEN 98%" OF YOUR PERSONAL POWER…AND WHY MOST PERSONAL DEVELOPMENT PROCESSES ARE INCOMPLETE OR DEAD WRONG

Chapter 1:

"The Discovery That Changed My Life… And Allowed My Wife to Eat Pizza Again…"

The "download" came in the middle of the night.

I was lying in bed and, unusually for me, I couldn't sleep.

For months, I'd been studying and trying every process I could find to help my wife overcome her gluten intolerance.

I know.

An intolerance to gluten doesn't seem like a big enough issue to keep one awake at night.

It certainly doesn't seem big enough to lead to one of the biggest discoveries of my life, and something that has literally changed the lives of thousands of people and businesses for the better.

Sometimes my Higher Power works in mysterious ways.

If you understood where I came from, and what my wife and I were experiencing at that time in our lives, it may not seem so strange after all.

To explain, I've got to start at the beginning.

I've been involved in natural healing and the power of thought (and basically all the "woo woo" stuff, lol) since I was 2 years old, which was when my dad had a dramatic career change. My dad broke his back on the job and the doctors told him he would never walk again.

He refused to believe it, and instead went looking for alternative ways to heal.

After months of research and hard work, he slowly crawled his way back from paralysis and eventually not only walked, but ran, worked, canoed, and played just like any other dad, with me and my siblings as we grew up.

What he learned impressed him so much that he became a clinical kinesiologist, which basically means he can test weaknesses in the body to find out what is going on inside and help people find healing. He taught my siblings and I everything he knew, which is why I can say I've been studying this for more than 30 years. It was an every-day part of my life, even before my pre-med degree in biology, study toward becoming a doctor of natural medicine, and numerous other professional qualifications.

One day when I was 12 years old, my dad invited me to sit on the couch because he needed to talk to me.

In my family, the only reason we ever talked was if we were going to play a game or if I was in trouble. My guard went up immediately when he asked to talk.

He sat down with me, he looked me in the eyes and said, "Tyler, your mom and I are getting a divorce." Up To that point, I hadn't even known that they had a problem in their marriage. As he looked me in the eyes and told me this, I got a sick feeling in the pit of my stomach. What I FELT him say, was that it was all my fault. He didn't actually say it that way, of course. But that's how my body interpreted it.

I hadn't been taught the skills of how to ask questions and clarify, so I put on a smile and pretended everything was okay. I just kept on pretending as my mom went through four more divorces, and my dad went through another one.

I became terrified of relationships. I knew that I was destined to fail. I just knew I could not hold onto a relationship.

More than that, I felt like I was to blame for each and every divorce. As the oldest son, I felt like it was my responsibility, and there must have been something I could do. I tried hard to be the perfect kid. I got straight A's, I became class president, I was the most valuable player on my football team, and I worked hard to excel.

Behind the facade, I suffered from depression and I never told a soul. I would literally sit on my bed and meditate on how I could kill myself, wondering if anyone would ever miss me. These experiences logically made no sense, but emotionally, and in my body, it became a pattern, a habit, almost as if it was the most natural thing that I could do. I became addicted to video games and pornography, and most of all, I was addicted to struggle.

Eventually, I cleaned up my act, and went on a 2-year mission for my church, afterwards I went to college. Overall, I was doing better, but I still had these deep-rooted feelings of fear, self-doubt, lack, and guilt for my parent's choices. Hence, I enrolled in spending literally hundreds of thousands of dollars and tens of thousands of hours on personal development, mindset work, breakthroughs, therapies, etc. that I mentioned in the introduction. I didn't want to be trapped in the same patterns and cycles that seemed like my destiny from my experiences growing up. I believed that there was a way to make a change for good.

Fast forward to the gluten intolerance experience with my wife. This gluten allergy had been an issue in her life for over 8 years, and she had repeatedly said how nice it would be to someday eat gluten again. I really wanted to help her.

I knew it HAD to be possible to overcome, based on my dad's career and the things I'd learned from him growing up. There are numerous natural healing modalities, including the law of manifestation/trapped emotions/root causes that claim to be able to remove food allergies and intolerances. I tried them all, one after another, on my wife. Some worked for a day or two, some didn't work at all. None worked for more than a week.

For some reason, this intolerance became an obsession with me. With all my years of experience and over 30,000 hours of working with my own clients in a clinical setting, it was beyond frustrating that I couldn't seem to shift a simple gluten allergy for my wife. I'm sure that deep inside, it was mixed up with all of my feelings of being not good enough, and being destined to fail, and wanting to ensure the success of my most important relationship. At this point in my career, I had stepped out of the clinic and was working as a business coach, helping my students enroll high-paying clients through their stories. We were making a comfortable multiple six-figure income, so financial reasons didn't affect my desire to pursue this idea. It just wouldn't go away! For six months, I studied everything I could get my hands on about allergies, intolerances, mind-gut connection, the effects of emotions and thoughts on health, how the body processes information vs. how the brain processes it, you name it.

Then, one night, the "download."

As I lay there, unable to sleep, a crystal clear picture of what to do to remove my wife's gluten intolerance came into my mind, along with the words:

"If you do it this way, it will work."

Now, I don't know about you, but when my Higher Power says something like that to me, I listen.

First thing the next morning, I said to my wife "Come here, I'm going to do this process on you for gluten."

She rolled her eyes. I'd been doing "processes" with her for months. But she agreed.

Ninety minutes later, she looked at me with wonder, and said "You know what, I think I want a piece of toast." While usually the thought of gluten made her cringe, all of that was gone, so she went and ate a piece of toast. No reaction. Later that night, she ate pizza. Still no reaction.

More than 3 years later, she still eats gluten without the slightest problem. All from doing one 90 minute process.

At that time, however, we still didn't know if it was a one-hit wonder, and with my background in science, I'm all about duplication and research. After a week or two of her being able to eat gluten, I set out to see how far-reaching the effects of this process could be.

At this point, I think it might be best to briefly describe why this process works, so your logical mind won't totally reject the mind-blowing stories I'm about to tell you about that happened next. Each of these stories is the true experience of myself or one of my clients, and you can find them in their own words at Alignmenteffectbook.com

The modern world has an obsession with the "mind." Everywhere you look, you can find information about the conscious and subconscious mind, how to attract what you want with your mind, the power of thoughts in the mind, how to get organized and be productive with your mind, how to form habits with your mind, how to get rich, happy, and healthy with your mind. (How many times have you heard that you just have to have a "millionaire mindset" or "think and you'll get rich"?)

When the modern world does address the body, it is usually in the form of an object to be handled - to be gotten into shape, to be worked out, to be fixed with surgery or pills, or to be healed with medicine and herbs.

I'm here to show you that it is the body, not the mind, that is responsible for a large portion of what happens and what we achieve. Of course, the mind is important in guiding the body, but the innate intelligence and physiological responses in every organ, gland, cell, and energy center of the body are ACTUALLY what create our results in every area of life.

Think about it this way: A human brain makes up around 2% of the weight of an adult person and cannot touch the world on its own. The other 98% of "you" is your body - the part that actually interfaces with the tangible world and the work you do every day. Attempting to change everything in your life by changing the "mind" is literally missing 98% of the equation!

Now, I know that this sounds totally crazy, especially if you have been studying the power of your "conscious and subconscious" or having a "success mindset" to try to achieve what you want in life.

My hope is that throughout this book, you will open yourself up to the paradigm that most challenges we, as humans face, are actually habits and responses stored in the body, not just in the mind. These responses can be measured and identified specifically down to the organ, gland, or energy center that is causing the problem. Unlike the mind, which seems to have an endless capacity to go in circles and create complexity; changing the body is simple, straightforward, and relatively easy.

I will explain how and why this works in more detail throughout this book. For now, what is important for you to understand, is that the reason what I do works so quickly and so permanently is that instead of trying to convince my "mind" of something through repetition and passion and mind tricks or whatever, I go straight to every organ and gland and energy center of the body and tell it exactly what to do. Then you don't have to "think" about making the change any more, the change is already made.

After shifting my wife's relationship with gluten, the logical next step, of course, was to see if it worked with other foods. With the health of our society today being the way it is, it was not hard to find four friends with allergies to soy, dairy, eggs, and peanuts respectively. I did the process with each one of them with the same result: They each came back to me claiming that they no longer had any negative effects from these foods, and what's more, they didn't even remember what it felt like to be allergic to these things. It was as if the allergy or intolerance never even existed for them.

Then I had another crazy idea. It is one thing to shift a relationship with food, which, all things considered, is relatively fluid and easy to change. At the time, I was in the coaching space, and I wasn't really helping people with food allergies. I was helping people with money issues. The people I was working with had a lot bigger problems than gluten and soy intolerances. They had money problems, relationship problems, and health problems. I had this crazy idea that this process (which I was beginning to call the "Alignment" or "Complete Alignment") could help them too.

Next, I tried it on myself. As I mentioned before, I had a decent multiple six-figure business, but it had been a while since I had people just come to me and ask to be my client, without my having to follow-up with them or hunt them down. So I "Aligned" to get every organ, gland, and cell in my body on board with having new clients come to me without me doing anything. And within 24 hours I had four different people reach out to me on Facebook, email, and Linked In asking how they could join my program, which turned into $8,000 in sales.

As a pre-med biologist, I'd studied all about the placebo effect. At this point, I was thinking "Wow, if this is placebo, I'll take it!" The scientist in me wanted to test this on other people who didn't have my bias.

I shared my story with my friend Bill, who is a very talented coach and healer himself. I did the process with him to have more clients come to him. He said that usually within a three month span, he'd have about ten new clients. After he aligned, he had ten clients come to him out of the blue in *one week*, without doing any marketing. By simply shifting energetic push and pull responses in his body, he was able to achieve his 3 month goal in 7 days.

I thought, okay, this is really cool. It works with food. It works with money. At this point I was kind of just playing around and wondering what else I could accomplish for myself and those around me.

It was then, I had the experience that convinced me that what I had been given was not just for me and my clients, but for as many people as I can reach.

I met a man named Craig at a conference where I was speaking. Five years before we met, he had had a cardiac arrest and had suffered with disabling symptoms for the entire five years. He could only function for four hours a day. If he went for a walk and looked to the left or the right, he'd fall over. He had to wear sunglasses and earplugs because his body couldn't handle the light or sound input.

Craig had been going to doctors and had tried all the medical routes for his symptoms, but nothing seemed to work. His wife was also a master practitioner in a number of alternative healing modalities, and had used everything she knew to help him, but without results. It seemed to them that this would be something that would be with Craig for the rest of his life.

As we talked, I thought to myself, "Theoretically, the only reason he had these symptoms is because some part of his body has a physical pulling response that is holding on to them (I call these addictions – more on that later) and pushing response to what he wants (I call them allergies). The alignment process can help with that.

Without thinking too much about it, I offered to do a session on him. I wasn't sure what would happen, but I thought maybe it would help him deal with his challenges better or something. I asked him to give me a call after a few days to update me on how he was doing.

Two weeks later, he called me in tears.

He said "I don't know what you did to me, Tyler, but my life has totally changed since that session with you. I am able to work 8 hours a day. I don't have to wear sunglasses or earplugs anymore. I can go for walks without falling over. You've given me my life back!"

That was the moment when I knew I needed to get this message out to the world. No more repetition and passion, no more getting to root causes, no more taking years and hundreds of thousands of dollars to try to create a change, it's time to Align.

Chapter 2:

"Everything I Thought I Knew About Personal Development Was Wrong...And Here's Why"

Ok. I get it.

At this point a lot of you are probably thinking, "Good stories, Tyler, but if this is so great, why isn't everyone doing it? What about people like Tony Robbins or Bob Proctor who have been changing people's lives for decades by working on mindset? How is this any different? And if working on the body is faster, why aren't they already doing it?"

Great questions.

First of all, they ARE already doing it. The body part, that is.

If you've ever been to a Tony Robbins event, you know that there is a lot of jumping around, high fiving, hugging, physically breaking through things, etc. Have you ever stopped to wonder why?

He, and every other great transformational teacher, already knows the power of the body. There is no way that their audiences would have the same experience if they all just sat in their chairs without moving or touching anybody the entire time. That's called school, and is it any wonder that kids grow up hating it?

For a change to be real, it has to move out of the mind and into the body. Or, for even faster results, move from the body into the mind.

However, in order to understand why Abundance Alignment is so drastically different from anything you may have tried in the past, it is helpful to do a quick overview of the world of personal development/mindset.

From my perspective, the majority of the things most "mindset" coaches do to help people transform fall into one of the following categories: Breakthrough, intensity and repetition, tricking the subconscious, habit or behavior modification, or releasing limiting beliefs/traumas/root causes.

We will examine them briefly.

First, Breakthrough:

Firewalking, ropes courses, breaking boards and arrows, getting on stage and shouting embarrassing or empowering words in front of a bunch of people. All of these are part of the "Breakthrough" ways people try to change their lives. In general, they are high emotion, high impact, and fun to experience.

The theory is that by putting yourself into a state of fear or excitement or hype, you open the door to your "subconscious mind" so that new messages can get in, and it works... sometimes... and the results last... sometimes.

I love going to events myself, and it's great seeing groups of people go through exciting experiences together and shift together.

The problem with this is that because these experiences are dependent on the energy of the moment, once the moment is over, most people go back to how things were before. They might have a temporary high, but they find themselves needing to go back again and again and for another high...

In other words, for most people, these experiences don't change what is really going on in the whole body. Just part of it. For a short amount of time.

Which brings us to the next category.

Second, Intensity and Repetition:

If you practice vision boards, affirmations, declarations, and many types of meditation, chances are you've been sold on the "Intensity and Repetition" school of thought for transformation.

The idea is that if you repeat something often enough and long enough, you will start to believe it. You look at images of your goals and dreams, say them, carry them around on a card in your pocket, visualize and think about them every day, shout them from the rooftops... you get the idea.

The intensity and repetition gurus say the point, again, is to convince your subconscious that you actually want the thing you want so it will make it happen.

Totally works. I used intensity and repetition to create my first six figures.

And it totally takes a loooonnng time.

I believe that for real change, you are actually trying to convince your BODY to change, not just your subconscious. If your mind repeats the thought enough, your body will eventually agree to come along for the ride.

Depending on your definitions, however, (we will cover these in detail in Chapter 6) trying to convince your body of something through intensity and repetition can actually make it take LONGER to happen in your life, and can even have the effect, by repeating the thing you think you want over and over, actually push it further and further away.

For real.

I will prove it to you over in Chapter 6.

Third, Tricking or Reprogramming the Subconscious:

This is an interesting one. Again, the idea is that your all-powerful subconscious controls everything in your life except for the miniscule amount of things you can control with your conscious mind, and if you can "trick" the subconscious into a new way of doing things, you will suddenly have totally different results. To do this, many people use hypnosis, altered states, shifting brainwaves, sleep programming, neuro-linguistic programming, rapid eye therapy, etc.

These processes have been really helpful to a lot of people. However, the issue with this school of thought is it sometimes makes change seem so mysterious and untouchable and esoteric, as if you have to get a doctoral degree to understand what is going on inside your own head. Since these processes are often presented as complicated, occasionally it leads people to believe that they can't actually change their own lives, or that something outside of themselves is actually controlling how they think and what they do.

Even if these processes eventually do lead to the results you want, they either take a long time, or are hit and miss. You could do hypnotherapy, for instance, one time and have a great experience and powerful shift, and then you could go back again and feel nothing. This is because again, you are only addressing 2% of who you actually are as a human being, and part of your body can actually form a fight/flight response to the therapy itself, negating everything you do after that.

I have nothing against these techniques. I've tried each of them and they do work. There is just an easier, faster, more user-friendly way.

Fourth, Habit and Behavior Modification:

There are tons of books, courses, videos, you name it on how to organize your morning, plan and execute your day, implement the six habits of success or 28 principles to become a millionaire or whatever.

Again, I love these books and ideas, and I use many of them in my life.

The challenge for most people is that these great ideas and principles become subject to "New Year's Resolution Syndrome."

You know what I mean.

You get the planner, set up the AM and PM routines, add reminders in your phone, create your schedule, and execute perfectly for about two days.

And then, most of the time, life happens.

Or more specifically, the allergic and addicted responses in every organ and gland in your body kick in to push or pull you away from what you want and towards the thing that they interpret as safe. I will explain this in detail in Chapter 4.

At this point, a lot of people give up.

A strong few continue to push through and keep doing the thing they need to do, but it feels like slogging through mud.

That's because your body is working full-time AGAINST what you are trying to accomplish.

You work SUPER hard, but don't actually get the goal, it takes way too long, or you do reach the goal, but sacrifice your health, family, or sanity. Your level 10 effort creates a level 2 result.

And you are left wishing that you had more willpower and a stronger "mindset."

Sound familiar?

Fifth, Releasing Limiting Beliefs, Blocks, and Root Causes:
Remember that time the bully in first grade called you a wimp and said that you couldn't play with the cool kids?

If you believe in the "releasing limiting beliefs/traumas/blocks/root causes" paradigm of transformation, could be the reason you now lack confidence and avoid people, which explains why it is so difficult to enroll new clients and ask for money.

The central idea is that all you need to do is find the moment when you made the decision to take on the limiting belief, trauma, block etc. and then reverse the decision or give yourself what you needed in that moment.

The theory is, once you find and release the moment of decision, you should be home free.

Or, once you find the trapped emotion or root cause, the symptom should go away and you should be able to now create the life you want without limitations.

As a trained Thai yoga therapist and Emotional Freedom Technique practitioner, I have put in thousands of hours and have seen people have amazing success through these methods. I've also learned a lot from others who have fantastic systems of finding and releasing trapped emotions and root causes.

However, from my experience, even these are limited because there are SO many "root causes" and experiences that make up each challenge we have. If you miss one, the challenge will come back. You could spend your entire life finding root causes and trapped emotions and digging into old traumas without getting to where you actually want to be. These tools are primarily focused on constantly removing what you don't want, and pain and negative symptoms, instead of simply tuning your body to what you DO want.

Also, for EFT specifically, although it does involve tapping on specific points of your body, and "neutralizing charge," it only covers a few specific points on the body and ignores the rest. As a practitioner, I would do many hours and as many as 14 hours on one topic to get it to shift. It was effective, but slow.

In contrast, once you align, the root causes no longer matter. They are shifted simply, systematically, and completely without having to spend hours delving into traumas and negative experiences.

I used many of the root cause tools in my attempts to help my wife get over her gluten allergy. They would work for a few days, and then they wouldn't. Alignment was permanent.

Each of these categories for transformation has it's pros and cons. Many of them do attempt to address the body as a whole, but they miss out on seeing how each and every organ, gland, and cell in the body isn't actually interpreting what you want or don't want. And because of that, it has to take longer to convince your body to change. You could be doing techniques that are positive. You could be saying positive affirmations. You could be doing meditation. You could be even going to therapy, counseling, or working on your physique. However, if part of your body is still holding on to a negative interpretation due to your past perceptions, then you will not see progress regardless of what technique you use. By far the biggest problem with each of the methods of change I've mentioned in this chapter is that your body can form its own fight or flight responses *to the processes themselves.*

For example, have you ever tried a tool or technique and it worked in one area, but then when you tried it another, all of the sudden the process lessened its value and you went to look for something else? Then that works for a little while, and slowly doesn't work either. This is how the personal-development junkie is created, the person who is always going to seminars and courses and reading self-help books, but without actually getting results. They've formed an addiction to self-help and an allergy to actually getting the help they need!

As I mentioned in the introduction, a few years ago I went through a personal development program that took five to seven hours a day, five days a week for almost a full year. I was also doing vision boards, declarations, and much more. And through that process, I learned that the mind is very powerful and you can change a lot through the mind, but if you only go at it through the mind, it does take hundreds and hundreds of hours. With a lot of repetition, focus, and passion. I was so tired of going through all the motions and having to readdress things and find all the things that were missed. It felt like this was the long route. I had done that for a long, long time.

When I started out in business, it took me 9 months to "manifest" my first $10,000 month working only through these mind methods. With Abundance Alignment, $8,000 came in less than 24 hours.

Hundreds of my clients and the clients of my Certified Practitioners continue to say they are achieving mind-blowing results with less effort and time than ever before.

Dr. Eric McEntire is a successful upper-cervical chiropractor in the Salt Lake City, Utah area. He had been my client when I was a business coach, and had been able to grow his practice to about $30,000 a month consistently. After losing touch for a while, we reconnected a few months after I developed the Alignment process. He told me he had been stuck at the $30,000 mark for more than two years, and nothing seemed to help him break through it. He had been investing heavily in marketing, networking, and professional development; and he'd been vigorously using many of the techniques we've discussed in this chapter for more than 2 years, but still had not been able to break through to his target income of $60,000 a month.

Based on the new understanding I'd gained from the Abundance Alignment, I thought, "Well, that means some part of him has literally become addicted to whatever it defines as $30,000. It might mean safety. It might mean security. It might mean, 'Hey, this, this is the only way I know.' And part of him has become allergic to the idea of increasing his income due to his past perceptions, something like 'It has to be hard work. I'm going to have to sacrifice more time with my family. I'm not going to be able to do it. It's too hard or complicated,' or simply 'It can't be so easy.'"

So, I sat down with Eric and did the full Alignment process. Within two days, he signed up an extra two clients at $5000 each, and within two weeks he had made an extra $30,000, bringing his monthly revenue to $60,000, which he maintained for months. From just doing one session.

Now before you go all crazy and start thinking that this is a magic bullet (or at the other extreme, dismiss it as being too good to be true), I need you to remember that Eric was already pretty good at the rest of the Unstoppable Success Equation (we will be covering this in depth in Chapter 8). He already had Skills, Work, and Focus. All we did in that one session was remove the allergic and addicted responses stored in the organs and glands in his body. Once he Aligned, he got the results *he should have been getting all along.* Read that again.

Remember, you could spend hundreds of hours in breakthroughs, intensity and repetition, diving into the murky depths of the subconscious traumas or root causes, or just go at it and hope that one day all your hard work will eventually get you results that you want.

Or you could Align.

Chapter 3:

"My Leaky House Revealed My Struggles in Business…And How Einstein Really Did Have All The Answers!"

Warning: Don't keep reading, unless you truly want to take full responsibility in every area of your life.

Now I know that for some of you, "responsibility" has a weight to it. This might be because you need to redefine (see Chapter 6).

For me, however, because I've aligned, responsibility is freedom.

Regardless of your definition or interpretation of the word, I am going to warn you that once you learn this knowledge, it's very difficult to unlearn. Once you open the door to a new lifestyle, it's very difficult to go back to your old patterns of struggle. Not that you would want to, but I do want to forewarn you that as you continue going on this journey, you might just let go of some identities inside of you that aren't serving you. At times it might be painful. It might be challenging. But it'll be worth it in the end, because on the other side is a gem waiting to shine.

When I first started using Abundance Alignment, I thought it was just a technique, another tool in my tool belt.

It turned out to be a whole way of living life.

It has literally changed everything --how I think, how I feel, how I communicate, how I see the world. It's changed who I am, my identity to the core.

Instead of settling or accepting what a person says is "true" or just "how it has to be" because that is how their life currently is, I challenge everything. I look at everything as just an interpretation, just a frequency and that frequency interpretation can change as easily as it was created.

Instead of avoiding things like I used to - hiding behind shame or guilt or struggle, now I choose to confront it and to embrace it. Don't get me wrong, sometimes I do give in and I want to hide in the corner, but it only lasts for a few minutes, whereas it used to last for months or sometimes even years.

As I have embraced the power of alignment, I never have to settle again. I don't have to accept defeat in any area of my life. I also don't have to sacrifice the things that matter most to me to get what I want. I see everything as a doorway to change.

For example, a few months ago, my family moved into a new house. Before purchasing, we had a professional house inspection. Our inspector went through everything really thoroughly and it was great. It was a great house and was everything that we wanted.

And then, after we closed on the house, and the day before we moved in, we were walking through, deciding where to tell the movers to put the furniture, when we found water leaking through the ceiling of the basement. The damaged area was so large that it covered several square feet and water was dripping on the floor below.

It was definitely a drop-in-the-pit-of-your-stomach moment, this was our brand new house! Luckily, the seller had simply made a mistake when moving out their washer and dryer and the leak was pretty easily fixed.

Then, after a week or two went by, I found another leak in a different spot. Again, not a good feeling for the new owner of a house.

In the past, I might have been frustrated, angry, and tried to find someone to blame.

This time, I thought, "Okay, if everything's a frequency and I am truly the creator of all that is in my reality, then I am creating these leaks. So where in my life do I feel like I am leaking out my energy? What is causing me to feel drained in my life that I haven't confronted or changed yet?"

As I asked those questions and started to align, I realized that there were some clients I needed to talk to. There was one that I needed to forgive, one that I needed to help step up and transform, and one that I just needed to let go of completely. They were leaks in my life. They were draining me. They were taking away from me.

I took care of the clients, healed some relationships, and you know what? The leaks stopped. My physical reality was a catalyst to help me find the thing that I wanted most, which was the freedom and the ability to create more impact. I wouldn't have found those if I didn't see it in the world around me.

If you are familiar with the idea of vibration and frequency, you probably already understand this concept, even if this expands its application. In the physical world, even though matter may appear to be solid, at the atomic and sub-atomic levels it is composed of very small components in constant motion or vibration. This vibration is different for different kinds of atoms, molecules, elements etc. and can be measured as a different, unique frequency for each. Similarly, in the meta-physical (world of mind, thought and emotion) domain, the component parts are in constant motion and can be distinguished by their unique vibrations or "frequencies."

To expand this idea, here is a passage from my first book, *The Enrollment Effect*:

> *I'm going to give you an equation that is going to completely alter your ability to get the results you want. It was founded by Einstein himself. This is an eternal principle that has lasted forever and will continue to last. It makes up the universe—including our successes and our failures. If you can get this principle, it will change your life. When I first learned it, I finally realized why my money wasn't where I wanted it to be, why my relationships were eluding me, and why I wasn't attracting high-paying clients. If I can get you to see, as I'm seeing, and visualize a bigger perspective; then as you go to make your impact and enroll clients, you'll be able to treat them differently and do things on a bigger level.*
>
> *This is important, so I need you to commit to focus on this. If you can get this principle, it will change your life. Clear all of your distractions and get present. You can quickly ground your-self by taking a minute to take some deep breaths in and releasing them.*
>
> *Are you ready?*
>
> *Write down this equation: $E=mc2$*
>
> *This is Einstein's law of relativity. Everything I'm going to teach you is based on this law. To better understand this, let's break down the pieces of the equation.*
>
> *The "E" stands for "energy." The Law of Conservation states that energy can neither be created nor destroyed; it can only be transformed from one form to another. This is important.*

The "m" stands for "mass." Basically, the mass of an object is a measure of the number of atoms in it—or in other words, a measurement of matter. What is matter? Everything that exists.

That means that everything has a mass, and is therefore a variable in this equation. Even your thoughts. In your brain, when you have an idea, there are things that are firing—protons, electrons, quarks—which create a process that can be measured. Think of an EEG, which measures brain activity.

The "c" represents the speed of light. The speed of light is constant and, for our purposes, all we need to recognize is that it's really fast. So, what is energy? Energy is mass sped up really fast.

From the equation, we know that if you increase the numerical value of energy, it increases the numerical value of mass. If you increase the numerical value of mass, it increases the numerical value of energy. What does this have to do with anything? Hopefully some light bulbs are starting to turn on.

If you want to increase the mass [or amount] of something in your life, you need to increase the energy you're putting in. If you want to increase the mass of the money in your life, increase the energy you're putting into it. Whether or not you're in a broken relationship is a measure of the amount of energy being put into it.

Your health, and whether or not you have dis-ease or are overweight, is a representation of the energy inside of you. Scientifically, there is a direct cause-and-effect relationship between energy and what is manifest, or mass.

> *You can change the numerical values in this equation at any time. This means that you can change everything fast. If you change the energy around your life, what you think, and how you live, the manifestations, or mass, of your life is also going to change.*

So, if there are leaks in my house, or my car keeps breaking down, or something comes up every time I start to move forward in life, it is a reflection of me. The "matter" that is showing up in my life is a reflection of my "energy" - or, the push/pull chemical reactions in my body.

The problem with most of us is that we go through life looking at everything that happens around us, but think that it has no meaning – it just is. We think it has no relation whatsoever to our individual life, thoughts, behaviors, experience, or way of being, but therein lies the fallacy. Consider the, perhaps shocking, truism that the only reason that "thing" would show up in your life is if some part of you was on board or in alignment with that thing, otherwise it wouldn't be there in the first place. Every single thing on the planet has a pattern of energy, of frequency, of vibration. Every mental, emotional, physical, and spiritual thing comes with energy. And that vibration only "exists" or is perceived in your life if you are on that vibration or frequency as well. This can be a tough pill to swallow, especially if you've created a life that is not ideal or if you have things going on that seem very difficult to change.

And I get that. Trust me, I've been through it and I've helped many others get through some similar feelings. But if you can look at things and say, "Wow, this thing is happening for a reason, I need to change. I need to change so that I no longer attract these types of situations." Then, you become a whole, a full creator and no longer do you feel at the mercy of, or a victim to anything.

That is why I appreciated those leaks in the house. Once I aligned and started to change my interpretations about myself and handle those situations, the leaks went away and I was able to have the things that I really wanted in my life again.

When I met Paul at a business conference, he was suffering from such severe back pain that he didn't think he was going to be able to endure his transatlantic flight back to his home. Because I've gotten used to looking for the connection between energy and results, I thought, "Well, the only reason you have this back pain is why? Because some part of you has literally become addicted to that pain and allergic to your ideal, which is freedom and the ability to move."

I agreed to do an Abundance Alignment session on him on a break from the event. As we worked, it came out that among many other contributors, his back pain was directly tied to finances. He had told me that due to the economy in his country, his business was a little wishy-washy and not as consistent.

After aligning, not only did his back pain go away, but within a week he had over $60,000 show up in his account from a previous transaction many months before that he had totally forgotten about. He didn't even know it was still there. When you align, positive things happen because your body is no longer fighting your results. Instead, it attracts and holds on to the things that you want.

Chapter 4:

"It's NOT 'All in Your Mind,' and How Chicken Nuggets and Green Peppers Prove It...The Truth That Lives Beyond Mindset"

Nearly all money blocks, self-doubt, limiting beliefs, procrastination, self-sabotage, and restrictions we experience as humans are caused by chemical patterns stored in the body, not just the mind.

This premise is a central idea of Abundance Alignment, and in this chapter I want to show you why I believe this is true, and how this paradigm shift is the one of the MOST important things you could do to take your life, finances, relationships, and personal fulfillment to the next level.

The easiest way to prove this to you would be to have you and I together in a room. I would ask you about your current biggest goals, and then I would "test" the strength and weakness of the different parts of your body to see how they respond. For a video of how this works, go to Alignmenteffectbook.com

For example, let's say that you really wanted to find a partner, the love of your life. You tried a bunch of dating courses, manifestation courses, online and offline groups to meet people, and you've been on a bunch of dates, but nothing seems to be working. You even have a description of your "dream someone" on the mirror and on a card you carry around with you and state out loud every day.

What you don't realize is that, even though your "mind" might be on board with this new partner, every part of your body is having a different response to your desire, depending on your past experiences and definitions. So even though you are "doing" all the right things, your body is having a physical response to counter everything you are doing: You get sick to your stomach when you go on a date. Your leg muscles tense up when you try to dance. You stumble over your words when you try to have a conversation. You move too abruptly or too slowly, and come off as either too aggressive or uninterested no matter how hard you try. You feel all these uncomfortable sensations in your body… because *THEY ARE ACTUALLY IN YOUR BODY!*

Then, you come to me. Because I understand Abundance Alignment and that every part of you actually has a different response to your goals, in just a few minutes, I am able tell you exactly which parts of your physical body are "on board" and which parts are having a fight or flight response to the idea of a new partner. For instance, I can tell you if your "brain" is sold on the idea, but your heart hates it. I can help you see if your liver interprets it as a threat, or your adrenal glands kick in a danger response when a new potential person even gets close. Your pancreas and gallbladder might be fine, but your small intestine can't handle falling in love one more time.

I can also show you how you can find all of these answers for yourself, without spending hundreds of thousands of dollars on advanced degrees and expensive machinery.

Yes, your "mind" can step in to try to calm all of these physiological responses, but by the time it catches up to what is going on, *they have already happened.* They happen immediately and without conscious thought because of chemical responses in every organ, gland, and cell of your body, and how they've learned to process stimuli independent of your brain.

Does this sound crazy?

Because western society is so "mind-" and "brain-centric," it may be hard to accept the idea that each part of the body has an independent response.

But just look at the studies.

For instance, the book *A Change of Heart* by Claire Sylvia describes the author's experience as the recipient of a heart transplant. She was told in the hospital that the donor was an 18 year old male who had just died in a motorcycle accident. Soon after that operation, she began to have some dramatic changes in her personality and preferences. Her favorite clothes changed. She became more of a risk-taker. She wanted to drink beer, something she hadn't particularly been fond of before. She also found herself with an uncontrollable urge to eat chicken nuggets and found herself heading to KFC all the time. She started craving green peppers, again, something she didn't think that she liked.

She'd also had a recurring dream about a mystery man named Tim. She felt he was the organ donor, so she began researching obituaries to find him. She eventually found him in a newspaper published in Maine, and was able to identify that man who was indeed named Tim. She visited with his family, and they said that he loved chicken nuggets, green peppers, and beer.

If the brain controls everything we are and the results we achieve, why did Claire experience such dramatic shifts after a heart transplant? The physical heart she received brought with it its own preferences, responses, personality, and even allergies and addictions. In this case, it wasn't her mind informing her body, it was actually her body - her physical heart - informing her mind and changing her behavior and mental and emotional state.

There are even crazier stories, such as an eight year old girl who received the heart of another girl who had been murdered. Soon after, she began having vivid nightmares about the murder. After several sessions with a psychiatrist, it was concluded that she was actually witnessing the real incidents. She was able to give such detailed descriptions of the murder, the weapon, the place, the clothes, and so much more so that they were able to convict the murderer for more details and other stories you can find them in the Book *The Heart's Code* by Paul Pearsall, Ph.D.

When I studied Ayurvedic medicine and Thai Yoga therapy during my doctor of natural medicine coursework, we extensively covered what is called "cellular memory." According to the Northern and Southern styles of Thai medical massage, the body "remembers" trauma when it is placed in the exact body placement (position of head, torso, limbs etc.) matching the time of trauma occurrence. So, if someone was in a car wreck, the trauma was actually stored and held by the cells in the physical position the person was in during the wreck. In order to release the trauma, we were taught to move the person to the same physical position they were in when the other car hit them, for instance. In that position, emotions and sensations would come up that could not be accessed just by "thinking" about the accident. Once they released the trauma while in that physical position, they were able to be completely freed from lasting effects.

This was not a mental process. It was a physical process. By working through physical trauma, they were able to change how the mind perceived it. We were changing the mind by changing the body.

(Now, the only problem with that is that it took lots and lots of hours and a lot of work. Sometimes we would do 12, 15, 20 or more hours putting a person into different positions and then watching the emotions come up and arise. Even though the results were phenomenal, I still felt like there had to be a more effective way to do it.)

There are hundreds and hundreds of other cases that show cellular memory and how our experiences are not just in the mind, and that the body influences the mind sometimes even more than the mind influences the body.

This is important to understand as you're learning to align, because it's not just a mental process. It's not just repeating something over and over. It's not just visualizing or wishing or hoping. It's not even going into the subconscious. Instead, it is getting into your cellular memory and how your cells interpret the things that you want, or don't want. If you can understand this principle, then as you learn how to align, it will help you transform your life in ways that you never thought possible.

The next time something that is not ideal happens in your life, remember that your body has its own interpretation. All pain is a disconnection. If you have pain - emotional, mental, physical, or any other kind - it is a disconnection that is not just in the mind, but in every organ and gland and cell in your body. What's more, each part of your body has its own interpretation of the pain. It could lead to a "pushing" response. Or it could lead to a "pulling" response that happens over and over.

Either way, the goal is to identify that it goes beyond the mindset and into your body. And if you can align and change how your body responds, then those cellular memories stop having to repeat negative cycles and you can actually choose how your body responds to your situations inside and out.

Chapter 5:

"The ONE Thing to Understand if You Want Results Fast… and What Puke Has To Do With 10xing My Income"

Did you ever get a stomach bug when you were a kid?

I know I did.

When I was little, my grandma lived across the street and I used to go to her house when I needed comfort. She would always make me a cheese burrito and listen to me talk while I ate it. She was the one person who I felt like I could share anything with and she would always love me, no matter what.

Strangely enough, cheese burritos became kind of associated with her in my mind. Anytime I would eat one, I would think of my grandma.

Until one time, I got a stomach bug. I felt miserable and made a cheese burrito for myself, thinking it would help me feel better. Boy was I wrong.

I didn't even want to look at one, much less eat one, for months.

The funny thing was, my "mind" knew that cheese burritos didn't equal my grandma, but my body associated them with her. Then, after I threw them up, my "mind" knew that there was nothing wrong with cheese burritos in general. However, that didn't change the feeling of physical nausea and disgust when I looked at them.

Think back to a similar experience in your life. This is a very basic example of what happens when our body forms a physical response to something. Except some of these push/pull reactions don't fade away over time, like our response to throwing up. Some of them stay with us and trigger fight/flight responses in the different parts of our body EVERY time we come across that thing from then on. We call these responses allergies or addictions.

An allergy is a "pushing" response that can be measured in specific parts of your body. An addiction is a "pulling" response. Both are being triggered all day long in the different parts of your body and are the entire reason you experience self-sabotage, negative cycles, blocks, chaos, etc.

The one thing that I want you to do if you truly want to succeed faster than ever is realize that every single one of your limitations, distractions, avoidances, compulsions, tiredness, family drama, and even physical symptoms are due to the frequencies and memory that is stored in your body as allergies and addictions.

You have a desire in your heart that burns bright, and all day every day your body is interpreting it.

Sometimes part of you interprets what you don't want as something to run to and distract yourself within when life gets hard. That body part likes to take the easier path, craves those chemical hormones, and is addicted to them... and thus demands that you continue to produce them by default.

Other times your body is so repelled and repulsed by the idea of what you actually wants that it pushes away every action and everything that should work, so as to retard your process toward that thing.

This is why some people literally take 40 years, a lifetime, or several lifetimes to actually get close to their goal. It is not just about working harder, working smarter, putting in more effort, more energy, more discipline, or just breaking through. It is about getting your whole body to work for you instead of parts working against you.

When I first got started as an entrepreneur, I saw some other entrepreneurs who were super successful. They were multimillionaires who had a good family and were healthy, kind, loving, and spiritually driven. I thought, "I want to be like that."

Then I saw other entrepreneurs, some of them in my family, who seemed to struggle all the time. They would get divorced and not be able to truly be happy in their situations or circumstances.

What's the difference? To me, it seemed like the ones who were thriving packed in a lot of experience in a very short amount of time, and the ones who are suffering and struggling took forever to get through the lessons and to grow.

So I tuned in and decided to have a prayer. My Higher Power is God, so I prayed and said "Okay, God, I want to have 40 years of experience in one year. Will you give it to me?" I was very sincere. It wasn't a joke or vain request. I was really ready and committed to do whatever it took to go through 40 years of experience in one year.

And what happened was amazing.

The year before I had really struggled. I was newly married. I was working with low-paying clients in a clinic, barely able to make ends meet. I went door-to-door to 26 different businesses in 2 days trying to get clients and was rejected by all of them. It was tough. I went through hell and back again. My addictions were coming up, my struggles. Even though I worked on myself daily with the repetition and the passion tool and tried to get to root causes, it didn't seem to be helping. And at the end of the year, I think I made a total of $12,500.

The following year, after my prayer, I was led to learn skills and to the right people and was able to create over $135,000, more than 10x'ing my income. I felt alive. I started writing my first book, the Enrollment Effect, and did some incredible things, including getting my wife her dream grand piano. I thought it would take five years, but I did it in one.

I share this not so you can see how great I am, but so you can see what is possible even if you are just getting started. What areas are you being stopped in right now? Where are you just getting by, not thriving? I can pretty much guarantee there are allergies and addictions related to this that can be easily shifted in a fraction of the time you thought might be required.

Another way to look at allergies, addictions, and alignment is to think about your goal as a target. You're looking at the target, you've got a bow and arrow or a gun and you're aiming down the barrel toward it. Growing up in Arkansas, this was something I did quite often.

The target is your goal. That's the thing that you desire.

Now, most people in life tend to do this: They take the gun and don't look down the gunsight. They just shoot at the target over and over with "repetition and passion." They shoot in the general direction and hope that they'll hit the target. And eventually, with enough repetition and passion, they actually WILL hit it.

What if they took time to align, which is putting the scope in its place and aligning it with the barrel?

Too often we just aim at our goals, and hope that someday our effort and positive thoughts will get us into a state of being where we will be able to achieve them.

However, just like in our example, if you take time to align before shooting, before putting in the energy and effort and working hard, then everything works in YOUR FAVOR instead of the occasional lucky hit. You save ammunition, you save energy, you save time by putting in effective work upfront instead of having to correct it at the end or repeat it over and over and over while guessing/trying different things which might work better.

It's not a perfect analogy, but I hope this helps give you an idea of what aligning could be like. And when you're struggling, just realize that whatever is going on is probably an allergy or an addiction, and if you take the time to align you receive much better results with less time and effort.

In real life, if your parents argued a lot about money when you were a child, you might have formed an allergy to abundance and an addiction to struggle. Even if you are already making a good income, you might suddenly find yourself unable to make more no matter how hard you try. Or, if you do get a little extra, something crops up in your relationship. Or in your health. Or something breaks down and you suddenly have extra bills. Because of the chemical reaction of stress you felt during your parent's arguments, your allergies and addictions could be triggering your adrenal glands, your stomach, and your shoulders, for instance. You either stay and try to push through and "fight," or you try to escape in flight.

Either way, it's not serving you. It starts taxing your other organs and glands. Your thyroid starts to be overworked. Your adrenals are functioning too much and producing too much cortisol and adrenaline, which in turn creates more of what you don't want. Your body moves into a state of constantly running from the thing that you want while holding on to what you don't want. No matter how much you work on your "mindset" about success, these parts of your body still put you into an allergic state where you PHYSICALLY experience stress until you finally give in and get rid of the extra money or success. This continues to happen until you pinpoint your allergies and addictions and put your body into a state of alignment.

My client Julie had a vision to go to Hawaii and create a thriving business helping elderly and disabled people thrive in an empowering environment. Julie is a go-getter. She is one to fire and then aim later. But the problem with this, is that what she wanted to create was so much bigger than her prior self.

Once she learned the power of the push/pull responses in her body, she realized that if she took the time to align to her goal first, she could attain it much faster without the struggle.

Within just a few weeks after becoming my client, she left to Hawaii (which was an alignment), found her ideal home just steps from the beach in the ultra-competitive 2021 real estate market (another alignment), and is getting and receiving the help she needs for her dream to become a reality (another alignment).

The last one is especially important because she had experienced some emotional and sexual trauma growing up and had trouble accepting help from others. After aligning this, the doors opened wide and she got the help she needed literally within hours.

Here are just a few of her messages to me through this process, shared with her permission:

"I aligned and found someone to do the work that I'm not good at"

"Today I aligned...a big win is another parent of a child with Down Syndrome is interested in my day program for kids"

"Today I aligned and for the first time I'm fine whether I hit my goal or not...that is a huge win...I also hit my lowest with weight"

"I'm so happy. Thank you for all you've taught. So much is hitting me for the first time now, but it couldn't have hit me if it hadn't been repeated and consistent"

Chapter 6:

"Why The Supercomputer in Your Body Doesn't Know What You Really Want (It's Not What You Think...Literally!)"

The first thing you can do to start achieving your goals 100x faster with the power of Alignment is to get crystal clear on what you want.

I know.

If you've been in personal development for any length of time, you've probably heard that about a million times: "Write down your goal. Get a picture. Visualize it in detail." etc.

Here is the deal. If you don't understand what I will share with you in this chapter, none of those visualizations and goal statements will be as effective as they could otherwise be.

In fact, in the worst case scenario, setting those goals and focusing on them is actually moving you further away from them.

Here's why:

It all comes down to definitions.

Almost always, if you aren't creating what you want or getting rid of what you don't want, there is a definition tied to it.

In the context of Abundance Alignment, "definitions" are "triggers" or "working labels" you associate with or place on a summation of your physical, mental, emotional, and spiritual perceptions of what you've seen, heard, felt, experienced, read, listened to or been told.

These interpretations or definitions are stored in your body. As we discussed earlier, some people call them cellular memory. They are interpreted differently in each organ, gland, and energy center of your body. This is why we cover them individually in the complete Abundance Alignment Technique, and why most personal development processes only give you a small portion of the results you could be getting with Abundance Alignment.

To give you an example of why definitions are so powerful in achieving your goals, let me share an example from my wife, Emily. For a long time, before learning about definitions, she struggled to be happy. She wrote about it, tried to clear it, worked on root causes, etc., all trying to help herself be happy. But it seemed like the more she focused on it, the less "happy" she felt.

Then, as we started learning more about aligning and definitions, she suddenly had a huge paradigm shift. She realized that intellectually she understood what "happiness" is supposed to mean. However, the way parts of her body interpreted happiness was completely different than what her mind thought it should mean. Because of what she'd seen and heard throughout her life, along with thoughts, feelings, and experiences tied to the word happiness, especially as a child, her definition of happiness was "Everything is perfect and nothing ever goes wrong."

Therefore, every time she was saying declarations, visualizing, clearing root causes, and trying to create happiness in her life, what her body actually HEARD her saying was "Create a scenario where everything is perfect and nothing is wrong"... over and over and over again.

You can see where this is going...

Since we are mortals living on a mortal planet, it is physically impossible to have a life where everything is perfect and nothing ever goes wrong.

According to her definitions, it was factually impossible for my wife to be "happy."

The more she tried, the worse she felt!

The thing is, until we started to understand the power of definitions, she had no idea that all of her success and empowerment tools were literally setting her up for failure.

She had no idea that her body was trying to create an impossible scenario when she asked for happiness.

Then she couldn't understand why she felt burnt out, exhausted, and stressed all the time.

Some of you may be thinking at this point: "Isn't our body and 'innate intelligence' or 'higher self' smart enough to know what happiness actually is and bring it into my life, regardless of past experiences or definitions?"

Consider this illustrative example.

Think of your body as a super advanced computer. You input the program of "I want to be happy." You focus on it enough that it moves out of your head and into your body. So, each organ and gland and part of you goes and opens its files on "happiness."

And this is what they find:

Your heart pulls out the time that your mom said "You're not going to be happy when you grow up unless you learn how to clean your room!" Therefore, happiness equals clean room. And not just any room, one that is perfect according to mom's specifications.

Your liver pulls up the time that you got super angry at your sister because she broke your favorite toy, and you yelled "I'm never going to be happy with you around! You always ruin everything!" Therefore, happiness equals nothing going wrong.

Your adrenal glands pull up how stressed you feel every time you try to make things perfect and "not wrong" in your life, and floods your system with adrenaline and cortisol, making you even more stressed...

Is it any wonder, then, that when you test your heart, liver, and adrenal glands in relation to the word "happiness" that they actually go weak?

The innate intelligence in your body IS smart enough to give you what you ask for... as long as it actually KNOWS what that is.

Holistically redefining personal definitions, so that when your mind says, thinks, or intends "happiness" your body understands it the same way, is the first step on the alignment journey.

Until then, your mind is literally speaking a different language than the body where 98% of your results occur. Without effective, aligned definitions, you're only using 2% of your capacity for change.

Let that sink in.

Now imagine what might be going on as your body's interpretation of love, money, friendship, a million dollars, freedom, marriage, a promotion, your business, kids, your spouse...

Yikes.

When you write your goal statement or get crystal clear on what you want, you might be writing and saying all the right things...but giving your body all the wrong ones.

As you come to understand this concept, a whole new world will open up for you. You will see why you've created certain results in the past. You will see why things that used to work for you no longer work, and what to do about it. You will understand why you seem to keep getting in arguments with certain people in your life - do their definitions match yours? You may even start to see world events and social issues from a whole new light. After all, every person and culture has their own definitions of words like "freedom," "safety," "capitalism," "government," and many more. Maybe the first steps to healing are simply to redefine definitions.

To further illustrate the power of definitions, especially in relationships, consider this story. When my wife and I were working toward our first Two Comma Club Award from Clickfunnels (if you aren't familiar with it, Clickfunnels is an online software company to help entrepreneurs launch marketing funnels – you can find out more at [Alignmenteffectbook.com)](Alignmenteffectbook.com) we reached a point where we were almost there, but things seemed to be stagnant. To receive the award you have to do over a million dollars with one funnel or product online.

We had made seven figures offline before, and we were excited to join the "club" online as well. But like I said, we'd been working really hard, and were getting ready to finish the $1 million and apply for it, but for some reason I just kept dragging my feet. I just didn't seem to have the drive to get over the last little hump and actually receive the award. My wife, on the other hand, was super driven. She kept saying "We need to finish the award!" and I'm like "Screw the award. I hate awards!"

It was actually beginning to cause a little friction in our relationship, so we did what we always do, which is align.

The first part of aligning is redefining, so we mapped out what the Two Comma Club Award represented to each of us.

And of course, come to find out, part of the interpretation of awards in my body was definitely not serving me. I wrote down things like "Awards are for the weak. Awards are ways that people who don't know you invalidate all the hard work that you put in because they don't care about you as a person. They don't understand you and what you've been through, and instead they give you a little plaque to represent all the pain they don't care to understand."

Pretty unhelpful definition, right? You'll notice though, that none of this made sense at the moment. Logically, I wanted the award, and I certainly didn't believe that Clickfunnels was trying to invalidate me. However, even though my mind didn't believe them, these interpretations in my body *were* actually preventing me from receiving the award.

Behind these feelings were interpretations linked back to when I was a kid and didn't feel loved or understood. I felt frustrated with people saying things, doing things, or giving me things to try to ignore the truth that was deep inside. It was almost as if they were trying to use the award as a replacement for love. For years I had avoided getting awards. In fact, when I graduated from college I literally skipped the graduation ceremony because it represented an award. I had dyslexia back then, and for me, college was so hard. I wasn't very good at memorizing, and I had difficulty with tests. I had a lot of these symptoms that I didn't realize were allergies and addictions that made it so I was the one who always had to study more and yet really struggled. And the "award" of graduation just seemed to negate all of the hard work I had actually put into my study. In a way, it felt like a slap in the face.

To my wife, however, awards represented validation. They represented a feeling of excitement, love, and of feeling like she was good enough. Growing up, she received praise when she got awards. It made her feel like she deserved it, she earned it, she's credible and real. Awards meant that she belonged with all the other people.

My wife and I had opposite definitions, and even though my wife's definitions seem to be more "positive" than mine, they weren't really serving either of us. More on that in a minute. With these opposing interpretations of the Two Comma Club award, we had constant tension toward each other in going for this goal. I would procrastinate. She would push harder. I would go do something else, then she would try to force it. It was like we were fighting each other while we were supposed to be working for the same thing, and we were getting nowhere.

Then, once we redefined, we gained a deep understanding of why I had felt this way and why she felt that way. No wonder why it was taking us so long to get the award! Redefining changed how we saw each other and ourselves. Then we aligned, and within a couple of weeks we finished the application and received the email that we had qualified for the award. Aligning is so amazing. It can work in so many different ways and it all starts with the definitions or our body's interpretations of what's actually going on.

One other note. As you redefine, I'm going to invite you to get out of thinking of black and white, "positive and negative" thinking. Your definitions might use what you consider to be "positive" or "negative" words, but what really matters is some are serving you and some are not. To your body, there are only the interpretations of push, pull, and aligned.

For instance, in the above example my wife defined "awards" as what seems like a lot of positive things - love, belonging, acceptance. However, in reality, this definition wasn't actually serving her either, because she was depending on the award to GIVE HER love, acceptance, belonging etc. If I was allergic to awards, Emily was addicted to them. Neither one actually helped us create what we truly wanted.

Now, I will help you start the basic process of redefining. It's very simple, and super powerful if you do it right. Even though we redefine as we prepare for a full alignment, redefining is a whole process by itself which can lead to potent shifts. It changes how you think and how your body reacts to what you are dealing with. To see how this looks live, go to Alignmenteffectbook.com

As an example, one time I took a client through redefining the word "debt." He had so much negative energy, so much charge, so much anxiety, fear, and even hatred towards that word. Because he was "in debt," he just kept creating anxiety, fear, and hatred in his life. No matter what he did to try to get out of it, he seemed to always accumulate more or take a really long time to make progress. Obviously not ideal experiences. All we did for him was redefine the word "debt." We didn't even align for this, but once we redefined it, it gave him a sense of freedom and liberation. He was actually able to get out of debt much faster.

As I describe it, I encourage you to take the time to actually go through this process. If you are listening to this book, pause the recording and do it too. If you are reading, take the time to actually do it. Redefining is a way to prepare for the Alignment technique. If you experience it by actually doing it right now, everything else we cover in this book will make a lot more sense. Again, aligning is a journey. It does take time and practice. But if you put in the time in practice, it's going to save you thousands and thousands of hours over the long run.

To help my client redefine, I first had him grab a piece of paper and draw a line vertically down the middle. On the top of the page, we wrote the word "debt." For you, it might be "love," or "money" or something else. On the left side of the page, draw a negative (minus) sign. On the right side of the page, draw a positive (plus) sign.

When filling in the sides, it doesn't mean that the words used are either negative or positive. It just means that your non-ideal definitions go on the left side while your ideal definitions go on the right side.

While working with my client, I asked him "Okay regarding debt, what are your perceptions, thoughts, experiences, feelings, what you've seen, what you've heard, what you felt that aren't serving you regarding debt?"

He started to share: "I feel like I'm a victim. I feel stuck. I feel like I'm always owing someone. It sucks. It's a trap. It's impossible to get out of. I'm always in it. It hurts. It's painful. I hate myself."

As he listed these definitions, I wrote them on the left side of the page under the "negative" sign. And the list went on and on and on.

If you are doing this yourself, the key is to thoroughly exhaust the list. When you think you've mapped out enough, then keep asking yourself, "What else? What else? Is there anything else?" You want to redefine thoroughly, so keep going until you exhaust ALL of the non-ideal perceptions. Essentially, these are addictions. These are the things your body has become used to and that are your current reality which is not serving you. Your body is literally creating chemical hormones based on these definitions and it has become so accustomed to them that it actually feels safe with them and is trying to protect you from change.

As you map this out, be aware that when redefining something really tough, you might feel bad inside. You might have physical reactions come up and that's okay. Later on, I'll show you how to change those reactions, but for now, know that sharing and writing "limiting" things down, doesn't reinforce them. In fact, it helps you conquer them by taking the first step in identifying them. Okay? I'm going to teach you how to align so that you can actually change the physiological responses that your body has towards these addictive behaviors you've chosen to accept. You probably don't think that you chose them, but you actually have, and we want to break that pattern and help you get your "non-limiting" choices back.

So back to my client, we mapped out all of the non-ideal feelings, thoughts, associations, what he's seen, what he's heard regarding debt, including phrases, like his parents telling him, "Don't get into debt," or "It's not spiritually advantageous to be in debt." All the stuff that he's read or heard that isn't really fully serving him. By the time we finished, there were more than 100 things on the left side of his paper.

Then I asked, "Ideally, how do you want debt to feel? How do you want to think about and perceive debt? What would be the most empowering for you?" And so we went on with the list on the right side of the paper.

He said "I want it to feel freeing. I want it to feel like I'm capable. I want it to feel like debt doesn't keep me in. It's liberating. It's a blessing. It's a way for me to get more of what I want. I can pay it off really quickly. It's a strategic and intelligent way to grow a business. It's exciting. It's simple to pay down. It comes and goes really quickly. It's a choice."

We exhausted that list as well, asking "What else? What else?" every time he thought he was done. By the time we actually finished his list, he had a paradigm shift. His past perceptions had been changed in such a way that it altered how he thought and felt and acted. And he looked at the word debt now with a completely different feeling and a different thought. He said "Wow, what if I just started to choose to create what I want instead of being a victim to what I don't want?" And very quickly after that, he WAS able to create what he wanted financially.

Redefining is a simple, simple process, and it is easily misunderstood if not applied to the fullest level. So I encourage you to practice. Take one word, something connected to your most important goal right now. You might choose money or love, health or sex. You could do "positive" things, or ones that you consider to be "negative." I've helped people redefine pornography, video games, and food. I've helped people redefine marriage and parenting.

You can even redefine yourself. Write out your name, all the past perceptions, painful associations and things that aren't serving you, and then map out who you really want to be. That is by far one of the most powerful redefining processes you can go through.

Not long ago, I did a group Alignment (which I do weekly with my higher-level clients) where we redefined intuition and trusting ourselves. This was HUGE. Most people had the feeling that they couldn't trust themselves. They were lied to, manipulated, hurt, or victimized, or their expectations were crushed. They felt like they weren't in tune. They felt that if they made a mistake, they weren't worthy of connecting to intuition. The list went on and on and on. We literally spent almost two hours redefining what intuition and trust meant. We switched the definitions to "Intuition is a choice. It's easy to tap into. I can do it whether I'm 'worthy' or not. I can trust myself to receive answers for myself. It's fun. It's exciting. It's transformational. It gets better and easier with time. The more I practice, the better it gets."

When we were done, people came alive. They were so excited to start trusting themselves and trusting other people more, and over the next couple of weeks I received tons of messages from them sharing the amazing things that were happening in their lives because of the new way they saw themselves and their ability to tune in.

The power of redefining is so, so cool. I want you to be able to experience it. As simple as it sounds, going through the process and really exhausting each list gives you power over the real issue, whatever it is for you at the moment. It's very difficult to change something that cannot be measured or seen. This process brightly illuminates the underlying problems by exposing the corresponding reactions to it, which are mainly allergic and addictive responses. This process helps map out the situation so that as you do the full Abundance Alignment Technique, your body will respond differently to those fight or flight impulses, and replace them with enabling, coherent actions instead.

So do it. Take some time, pick a word and redefine. If you want more on the redefining process, you can go to Alignmenteffectbook.com to experience it for yourself.

Chapter 7:

"Why 95% of your problems can actually be changed...and the other 5% can too"

Now that you know how to redefine definitions, the next important step is to use that knowledge to identify the push and pull reactions in your body that are shaping what you experience every day of your life, even though you have no idea that they are there.

To a large degree, most human beings go through the motions, accepting things as they are without challenging them or looking to see if there is a more effective way. They use thoughts and words without realizing how their body is interpreting them, and then wonder why they are getting the results they are getting in their lives. Because you are reading this book, you already know about your personal power and think outside the box, and you have probably already achieved high levels of success in many areas of your life. You can do even better by removing disabling unconscious inhibitors produced by and in your body.

Too often, we believe something just because we're born a certain way or because someone says something is a "scientific fact." Our body believes it too.

In the past, it was a "fact" that the world was flat. And that was a fact that DNA could not be altered or changed. It also used to be a fact that flying was impossible, yet here we are in a world where flying is simple. It's super easy to do. As new ideas, research, evidence, and invention comes out, we learn and acquire new,more powerful and enabling ways to do

Note: as you read this chapter, remember that the things I describe here are personal experiences. I don't have a medical degree and nothing I teach should be construed as medical advice. I don't diagnose or prescribe anything. Always consult a doctor before you make medical decisions for your family.

When I was growing up I was told that I had asthma. It felt real to me. It was my identity. It was my addiction. I was asthmatic in fourth grade. I remember one time I was playing soccer and then all of a sudden, my chest locked up on me and I couldn't breathe. I was wheezing and hacking, and I couldn't get any air. I didn't know what was going on. It was hard and frightening. My teachers called my parents and told them I was having an asthma attack. From that point on, I believed that I had asthma and that it was difficult for me to breathe or run long distances. It became my reality. My body believed it as "fact." It held on to the idea that I was asthmatic and that asthma was difficult to change.

However, because of my dad's example in overcoming paralysis, as I grew older I began to challenge this belief. I started to work on myself and change my habits, I began to take certain supplements that were designed to help improve my condition. I worked on my mindset. Even after doing those things, it still felt like my body was fighting to hold on to my asthma. I felt progress and changes, but some part of me still felt the resistance to being able to breathe.

So, I studied how my body responds to certain allergens out in the air. I used tools to help me strengthen my lungs and practiced holding my breath. Because I held to the belief that asthma was no longer my "fact" I practiced until I could hold my breath for several minutes, and eventually was able to run a full marathon without any breathing problems at all. Today, I don't even think about myself as having asthma. Looking back, I realize that the physical symptoms the doctors told me were "uncurable" were actually allergies and addictions held in my body that could be changed.

As you go through your life today and this week, start to notice the things that seem to be a "given." Do they actually have to be that way? Do you have to have that health challenge? Do you have to go into a negative cycle again? Do you have to have that allergy? Is there a relationship or family problem that just keeps repeating itself over and over? What about that income ceiling you can't quite break through, or the thing your team hasn't been able to fully understand or implement?

Take a moment to start brainstorming the things in your life that you want to change. Try re-framing or thinking about these as possible allergies and addictions that are creating seemingly un-ending, unpleasant or unwanted situations or conditions? Write them down.

Similar to Newton's third law of motion, "Every action has an equal and opposite reaction," for every allergy, there is an equal and opposite addiction -And vice versa. So if you struggle to make friends, for instance, you not only might have an allergy toward belonging, but you also probably have an addiction to feeling left out. The way to eliminate them both is to align. This is another reason why Abundance Alignment is so much more powerful and effective than other personal development processes. With other techniques, even if you find the root cause or break through your "limiting belief" that no one likes you (addiction) you still have the allergy that pushes away being loved and accepted. The allergy has not yet been addressed. That is why crazy things often break loose in one area of your life just at the moment you start to have success in another area.

This is ninja-level stuff. If you start to really understand it, cool things are about to happen in your life.

Another thing that is important to understand right now is the difference between what I call "Godly burdens" and everything else in your life.

For instance, I can just see someone reading this chapter and saying "Well, Tyler, what if I'm born with no arms? I can't just align and suddenly have arms, can I? It's just 'the way things are.'"

Great question! I look at aligning as having two parts. Burdens, meaning things that are hard and challenging, are mostly self-imposed. I'd say as many as 90-95% of the unpleasant things we go through are self-imposed. This includes what is happening in relationships, health, finances, all of it. If they are self-imposed, we can change them.

The other 5-10%, are "Godly burdens." Meaning, I believe that they were given by God or the Universe or whatever your Higher Power is, to help you grow and expand. I can't tell you what these are for you because they are different for everyone, but they could include things like being born blind or without a limb.

Here's how to tell the difference: Godly burdens *fuel you*. Even if they don't go away, they become something you use to make an even bigger difference in the world. If you align self-imposed burdens, you conquer them. If you align a Godly burden, it stays there, but it changes from a stumbling block or excuse to a tool to be used to accomplish everything else you really want.

Even if you have this kind of burden, you still aren't limited by it once you align.

In other words, you have the power to change pretty much anything in life. Especially the 95% of things that are self-imposed.

One example of this is my friend and coach Dana Dereks, who is a serial entrepreneur and the author of *The Dream 100 Book* (which is an awesome book, by the way. If you are an entrepreneur, be sure and check it out.)

In one of our conversations, Dana told me that he had a gluten intolerance, and had for years. If he ate gluten, he'd have digestive issues and other symptoms.

Now if you know Dana, you know he's done a lot of stuff. He thrives in his business, he has a good family, and has a fantastic lifestyle.

In this one area, he had just accepted the gluten allergy as a reality.

As we talked, I asked him "Is this something that *has* to be this way? Like if you could change it, would you?"

It had honestly never occurred to him that it was something that could be changed. There were times in his life that he felt like he didn't belong because of this gluten allergy. He felt ostracized because he couldn't eat what everyone else was eating. He couldn't go with his family to certain restaurants. It was annoying when everyone had to go out of their way for him. It affected his lifestyle, how he felt about himself and others, his social life, and much more.

After we aligned Dana, he sent me a picture with him eating spaghetti with his wife at the same restaurant they'd been to on their honeymoon. It was a really special moment for him.

It was awesome to see his transformation and that he didn't accept defeat in this area. Now he can eat gluten without any reactions. But more than that, he has a new perspective that he can literally change anything. He doesn't have to be a victim or resign himself to his "fate."

With proper alignment, consider what you could accomplish in business, family, or anything that you might be struggling with? What if you could remove the obstacles? Eliminate anything hindering your progress? What if you could change or see the "negative" as the opportunities in disguise which they probably are? What if the non-ideal didn't have to be real for you anymore? What would you do?

SECTION TWO:
THE SECRET PROCESSES THE GURUS DIDN'T WANT YOU TO KNOW

Chapter 8:

"The Unstoppable Success Equation...How to Get Anything You Want"

There is a simple formula to literally get anything you want in life. Remember, Alignment isn't a magic bullet. You still have to put in the work. It still requires effort. Alignment simply clears the way for you so that all the effort you put in actually moves you toward the result you want, instead of fueling your allergies and addictions.

Over the years when I've struggled with my relationship, I thought to myself, "I wish there was a handbook that I could just read that says 'Here's how to improve your marriage with Emily.'" When I had kids, I wanted a handbook to tell me exactly how to handle situations with my kids when things just weren't working. When I had problems with my marketing funnels or trying to grow my business, I wanted somebody to swoop in and help me figure out how the heck to get it all to work together and be profitable.

Well, I believe that there actually is a simple equation to success in any area of life or business that you want to achieve.

Here it is:

$$U = \frac{S(W+F)}{(A)(A)}$$

It is called the Unstoppable Success Equation (USE), and it has several parts.

The U is your "Unstoppableness," meaning your ability to achieve what you want in any given area in the least amount of time possible. The higher that number, the faster and more effective you will be at what you are trying to accomplish.

On the other side of the equation we have S, which stands for your Skill level, how good you are at the things you will need to do to get what you want. Obviously the more skilled you are in marketing and sales, the more money you will make. The more skilled you are in communication, the better your relationships will be.

When I first started as a massage therapist on my way to becoming a Doctor of Natural Medicine, the only skill I had was massage. If I got someone to actually become a client, I had the skill to actually work on them.

However, it was super hard to make a living because I didn't have the skill of marketing, selling, or enrolling clients. Once I learned these skills, I was able to actually make an income as a massage therapist. Without these skills, I would have still been stuck. Skills are essential to all areas of your life and business, including the skills of how to keep your commitment and follow-through, and the skill to communicate what you want to other people or systems so they can do things for you.

W and F stand for Work and Focus. If you don't yet have a good definition of "Work," you could substitute "action," or "doing." The main idea is that you are actually taking steps toward what you want, not just thinking about it. Focus means that you are putting concentrated effort without distraction. That is super important, because if you lack focus, you'll be all over the place and you won't actually create momentum or progress in any area of your life. Focus is needed in order to succeed, and work is always an element to the success equation. You have to put in the work. Even if you have hired it out and other people are doing it instead of you, it's still work.

So as you up level your skills, multiplied by work and focus, you increase your ability to be unstoppable in creating what you want.

But here's the caveat, the Skills and the Focus and the Work are all divided by your Allergies multiplied by Addictions. They are the number one killer of all your focus, your work and your skills.

This is why even if you have a lot of skill, a lot of work, and a lot of focus, it could still take you years to attain your goals. They are constantly being negated and "divided" by your allergies and addictions. For every step you take forward, your allergies and addictions take another step back. You are constantly fighting yourself.

Take a moment to consider the thing you want to create or change in your life right now. Now, rate yourself on a scale of 1-10, with 10 being the most and best in the areas of your Skill, Work, and Focus toward that thing.

For instance, maybe you want to have a better relationship with your son. On a scale of 1-10, you are about a 5 in skills. You are decently good at listening to him, but sometimes you tend to want to jump in and solve things before he is ready. You sometimes have a hard time with the skill of enjoying it while he talks about things that don't interest you.

You are really motivated to connect with him, so you schedule one-on-one time and rate yourself as a 7 on work. Sometimes, though, distractions come up and these special times are set aside, giving you a 3 rating on Focus.

The numerator in your equation, is 5(7+3), which equals 50.

However, as you learn more about allergies and addictions in your life, you realize that some things your son says or does are always triggering you. When you do spend time together, you can't enjoy it. You realize that because of how your dad treated you in certain situations, you formed an allergy toward closeness, and an addiction toward thinking about other things when people are talking to you. You rate both your Allergy and Addiction as a 7.

So the denominator of your fraction is 7 times 7, which is 49.

$U = 5(7+3)/(7*7) = 50/49 = 1.02$

Without getting too precise with the math - these numbers are simply subjective representations of your experience, not an exact science - you can see that 50 divided by 49 is not very much. Even though you are putting in a level "50" effort, your ability to create what you want with your son is closer to a level 1!

Is it any wonder that it doesn't seem like you are making any progress in your relationship?

At this point, most people either start blaming the other person - "He just doesn't want to have a relationship with me, and nothing I do seems to make any difference" - or they try to work harder on the numerator of the equation. They go to parenting courses. They set aside even more time for the relationship. They set reminders on their phone. They enlist other family members to help. They go to counseling. They try everything they can think of.

Yet, even if they raise their number in Skill, Work and Focus all to a 10 (which, by the way is very unlikely, because their allergies and addictions will be stopping them from doing that too), even if they raise them all to a 10 and their numerator is now 10(10+10), which is 200; they still aren't getting the result they deserve for the amount of effort they are putting in. They are still only getting about a "level 4" result (200 divided by 49), except this time it is for a level 200 effort! Then they get burned out, frustrated, and exhausted, and begin to think that there is something seriously wrong with them.

This is the pattern which many smart, capable, powerful high achievers fall into - If not in their business, in their relationships or in their mental or physical health. The dream of "having it all" seems more like an exhausting pathway to having nothing left.

However, you no longer have to be trapped by this pattern. You know better. Let's take the same scenario, and this time, instead of working on the numerator, we work on the denominator of the equation, the Allergies and Addictions.

So you are still trying to work on your relationship with your son. You still have a level 5 Skill, level 7 Work and level 3 Focus. However, you learn to redefine and align. Let's say you don't have time for a full alignment, so you don't completely eliminate the allergy to "closeness" and addiction to "thinking about other things when people talk to you." Say you only take these both down to a 5 each. 5 Allergy and 5 Addiction.

Now, you go to spend time with your son, and instead of a 50/49 result, you get a 50/25 result. Your 1 becomes a 2. You literally DOUBLE the result with the *SAME AMOUNT OF EFFORT*.

$$U = 5(7+3)/(5*5) = 50/25 = 2$$

Then, what if you took your level of Allergies and Addictions down to 1 each? This time you are getting a level 50 result, again with the same amount of effort you were putting in before!

$$U = 5(7+3)/(1*1) = 50/1 = 50$$

Can you see why Alignment is so powerful?

Is it starting to make sense why my client Eric was able to double his income in two weeks, without changing anything in his business?

All we did was help him stop negating the things he should have already been receiving, based on his Skill, Work, and Effort.

Once his body stopped working against his results, he was easily able to say, do, and act in a way that matched his true capabilities. Therefore he was able to start landing the deals and enrolling the clients he would have otherwise missed simply because of his allergies and addictions.

So the key here is yes, you do acquire skills. Yes, you work. Yes, you focus. But if you genuinely want to succeed as fast as possible, you neutralize and eliminate as many allergies and addictions as you can. I.e., you Align. The more allergies and addictions you have, the more it stunts and dilutes your skills, work, and focus - sometimes negating them altogether.

We all know those people who seem to be always working and never able to get ahead. Now you know why. It is not just about "mindset," and telling them so almost always just makes it worse. Until things start to shift on a cellular level through Alignment, you, and they, are just spinning your wheels.

If you do learn the skills, but are not applying them, that is likely an allergy or addiction. If you are working really hard without seeing corresponding improvement or results, that is also an allergy or addiction. If you improve in one area but sacrifice another, that is an allergy or addiction. If your focus is watered down, if you are distracted often, if you find yourself turning to food or porn or social media instead of putting in the work, that is an allergy or an addiction. The equation applies to not just your body as a whole, but to every organ, gland, and energy center. When you fully Align, you address each one of them and can achieve what you want easily and consistently without all of the circles, struggle, and things not working.

Change your allergies and addictions, change your frequency, change your life.

Chapter 9:

"If You Want Success, DON'T Do This! The Plague of Personal Development, Outsourcing, and Waiting"

Almost $10 billion is spent every year on self-help, personal development, and mindset

Out of that $10 billion, a shockingly few "self-investors" ACTUALLY get results.

You know why?

As discussed throughout this book, hardly any of the courses, books, and seminars address the body as a whole. They just talk about the mind, habits or root causes. They miss out on the other 98%. Ignoring the critical role of the body gives only a 1 in 50 chance of success. Big mistake.

Plus, they don't cover Allergies and Addictions, and their deleterious impact on results. And they certainly don't tell you how to Align every organ, gland, and energy center in your body with what you want.

As an Abundance Aligner, you DO get results.

I'm going to share with you three things that you ABSOLUTELY MUST NOT DO if you want to achieve the life of your dreams and get your goals 100x faster than ever before.

First, Don't Become a Personal Development Junkie.

Seriously.

This is coming from a guy who helps people change for a living.

Don't get me wrong. I love personal development. I love to read books, go to seminars, and learn about the power of the mind. I get super excited when I discover new theories, philosophies, science, tools, and ways of doing things.

However, I see too many people turn this into a way to *run* from life, instead of a way to *create* their life.

It's almost like they go through a whole bunch of courses and processes and start to feel better, but underneath they don't actually feel better, but they think they should feel better, so they have to go to another event or buy another course to make sure. They try to justify their feelings of being unhappy by getting motivated for a little while, and then they need another fix.

It's actually a very addictive cycle. They get one thing, feel a momentary high and endorphin release, get motivated temporarily, then find another and keep spending, spending, spending.

It's kind of like a social media addiction, but a lot more expensive. They get a "like," and it gives that sense of accomplishment. It's almost like another life, but it's a false one and it doesn't actually lead to lasting results. I suppose this type of addiction is much better than drinking alcohol or smoking, but still.

Whew.

Personal development junkie-ism happens because people never actually get to the core of their "problems" in the first place. I used to be there. I see a lot of people go through personal development, raising their expectations really high, doing vision boards, affirmations, and they get excited, they get motivated. They feel different. They think it is starting to change who they are, but then in reality, their results stay the same. They have all these high expectations, all these goals and aspirations and boom, they fail. They fall short and now they form negative interpretations and feelings toward the thing that could have helped them. Because it didn't get what they wanted, they have connected a negative or "not ideal" definition to that effort. Now every time they use that method, their body actually fights against it.

It's kind of like what Stephen Covey shares in his landmark book, *The 7 Habits of Highly Effective People.* You are trying to find your way around one city with a map of another city. You are completely lost, but with a "positive mental attitude," at least you are motivated.

Instead of going through this self-inflicting pain of repetition and setting yourself up for failure, you can protect yourself by realizing that every single word has a frequency and definition in your physical body. Yes, personal development can be great, but instead of using it, abusing it, hating it, and forming negative interpretations around it, why don't you change how your body interprets those things, then let them work for work for you instead of against you.

We covered this in Chapter 6, but it bears repeating now.

Let's say I'm doing an affirmation "I'm a money magnet."

My reality is I'm not actually making money. I feel like money sucks and I'm not making money. I keep putting in more passion, more focus, and repetition into "I'm a money magnet. I can receive money. I can make money." Every time I say it, what my body really hears is "You suck at making money. Money is hard. You lose money when you make it."

If those are my definitions, every time I say that positive affirmation, I'm actually reenforcing the negative reactions inside of myself. It's like someone punching themselves in the face over and over and over and smiling the whole time, which gets them nowhere.

After that, I'm still broke, and still unhappy, and I go find another event or technique that I think will help me, but all it's doing is feeding my allergy to real change and addiction to personal development!

Don't do that.

If you catch yourself heading that direction, redefine and align right away. You will save yourself years of struggle and tons of headaches.

The real purpose of personal development is to go and DO the things you need to do IN REAL LIFE, so that you can become who you want to be and achieve real, tangible results. That's it. If your personal development habit isn't getting you those things, it's time to find another direction. Or even better, align to your habit so it works for you instead of against you.

I've done so many processing techniques. I've spent almost half a million dollars and literally tens of thousands of hours on my personal development and transformation to grow myself into who I am today. Even though I am forever grateful for all that money and time that I spent and who I became, I now know that there is a better, faster, more effective way.

Second, Don't Outsource Your Problems.

Most high achievers love the idea of outsourcing and delegation so that they can get more done and live a more relaxed lifestyle. (Even if most of them struggle with actually letting go.)

This backfires, however, when they try to hire others to solve their personal problems for them without actually confronting them themselves.

There was a time when I wanted to build a sales team for my first coaching company. I felt super insecure about hiring people in general, and especially about hiring salespeople. So I found a lady who had built a successful sales team for one of my previous mentors, and hired her for a large fee. I thought that since she had done a good job for this other guy, she would be able to do the same for me.

The problem was, I didn't approach the transaction from a place of ownership. Instead of working through my insecurities, I breathed a sigh of relief that someone else would "deal with it" for me.

In other words, I hoped that this lady would be able to magically build me a sales team, even when I didn't confront my own allergies and addictions about hiring.

You can guess what happened. She worked for me for a full six months. And at the end of it, still no team, no extra revenue, and tens of thousands of dollars out of my pocket for virtually nothing.

Ouch.

A lot of people would have blamed the lady I'd hired. But I knew she was capable. Maybe she could have done a few things differently, but she'd helped my previous mentor build his business through a sales team and rapidly increase his business with success.

So why didn't it work for me?

Because I was trying to "outsource my problems."

My problem wasn't that I didn't have a sales team. My problem was that I wasn't willing to confront my own insecurities about having a sales team.

That being the case, no one I hired could have built me a sales team that worked.

This is a hard pill to swallow, especially if you have been burned by people that you thought would be the solution to all your problems.

The *real* problem is thinking that there is someone out there who can save you from the real work of facing yourself and changing your life from the inside out. I'll give you a hint: that person doesn't exist – Or rather, there is only one such person – you.

Don't get me wrong. I am a HUGE proponent of hiring coaches, delegating, and building teams. There is no way to create the abundant life I'm after without them. I've learned tons from every coach I've hired, even the ones who didn't "work out."

I've also learned to approach every situation with the understanding that in order to get the full benefit of what they offer, I need to make sure that my own mind AND body are on board. If things don't seem to be working out, I know I need to Align, and then I will be able to see clearly to know if I need to go a different direction. Hiring is great, but you must take full responsibility for it, and for yourself.

I hired my first $35,000 coach when I'd never actually made that much in a year. I made a decision that even if he DIED, *I* was going to make this program successful for me. He ended up being the coach that helped me go from $12,500 to $135,000 at lightning speed. I succeeded faster than many of his clients who were from much more affluent backgrounds and had tons more experience than I did. Why? Because I didn't outsource my problem to him. I knew what my weaknesses were, and the skills I needed. Even though I hadn't developed it yet, I applied all the pieces of the Unstoppable Equation. I knew that I was the one who was responsible for my results, so any time resistance came up, I ploughed through it. I did the internal work as well as the external work, and it paid off.

There've been times where I've hired someone to teach me a skill, but what I really needed was to feel confident in myself. There've been times where I hired out someone to help me with my emotional state, but I really needed some skills. Either way, the biggest thing I need is actually to change how my body interprets both skills and emotions.

Trust me on this one, if you hire stuff out - whether in family (someone else teach my kids to respect me, or make my wife happy), or in health (just take this miracle pill, or get this surgery, or go to this doctor and you'll be healthy) or finances (hire this dude and all your money problems will go away!) without applying the Unstoppable Equation and fully confronting the allergies and addictions that are creating the problem, it will simply come back to bite you again in a different way.

For instance, let's say you are running an online business and things just aren't working, or they're taking too long. So, you hire someone who knows what they're doing, which is great. However, then all of a sudden things don't feel like they're working with your marriage. Maybe your spouse is being more triggered or reactive or your kids just aren't following instructions. Drama starts to happen in your family life.

Many times this happens with clients before they come to work with me. They hired out a problem only to have it come back and slap them in the back, like a boomerang. They throw the boomerang and say, "Hey, here's my problem. Go solve it!" And for a minute, it feels solved. And then it comes back with a vengeance, just in a different area of their life.

Don't do that. Do yourself a favor and confront the things that you avoid. Recognize your allergies and addictions, see them thoroughly, and then align them.

Solve your real problems first, then outsource.

Third, Don't 'Do Nothing.'

Ok. This should go without saying.

I've worked with enough people that I've got to say it.

Doing nothing and hoping that your negative cycles, self-sabotage, insecurities, allergies, and addictions will magically fade away just doesn't work.

And just barreling through, working harder, turning to another business or productivity coach, throwing money at your family members, investing in the latest tech gadget or fad, running more ads, hiring another team member, or trying to fit more into your already crammed schedule isn't going to solve the underlying problem for you.

Sorry.

We like to think that time or some special circumstance will heal or change all, but allergies and addictions aren't connected to time. They're connected to interpretations.

One time, I was talking to a potential client who was looking into a program that I offered. He really wanted to make a change in his life, but he said "You know, I really want to do this, but the timing's just not right. I know I need to make a change. I see the power of what you have to offer. When I have the money set aside, when I'm ready, when I don't have so much going on, then I'll do it."

So he put it off.

A year later, I had the same person reach out to me again. As we talked, we both realized that he was in exactly the same place, financially and emotionally, as he had been the year before! It was as if nothing had changed, except he had another year of struggle under his belt. He said "Now I'm really ready. I've gone through all these different courses and I'm still not getting the result." He'd gotten addicted to knowledge and allergic to implementation. Finally, he decided to confront that response, move forward, and start to work on his life.

Waiting for things to magically change isn't the answer.

Moving forward and taking steps to confront what's real and then change it is the answer.

To recap, you must implement these three things if you want lasting success:

1. Don't be a personal development junkie.
2. Don't outsource your problems.
3. And Don't do nothing.

Your success matters to me. You've chosen the right book because I can help you bridge the gap between logic and emotion, address the body as a whole, and align allergies and addictions so that what you do actually works for you, and you don't have to waste precious time in cycles.

Change is possible. Let's make it happen.

Chapter 10:

"What to do Every Week if You Want Success...and How My Daughter's Fear of the Dark Can Get You There"

The best way for you to succeed long-term in this is to have a weekly check-in to see if you're still on focus and on track, and consistently look for what you need to align. Make it become a way of being almost like eating and sleeping and breathing.

When you allow Alignment to become a lifestyle, not just a technique or a process that you use once in a while, amazing things will happen for you.

Make it habitual, kind of like taking a bath.

Some people who set out to change their lives think, "I've worked on myself already. It should be completely done. And I never have to look at it again."

Well, that's like saying, "I've already taken a bath this week. I shouldn't have to take a bath ever again."

There's certain things that we just need to do consistently to grow ourselves. You can't expect to work out one time and become the strongest person ever. You can't expect to go on only one date with your spouse and have a thriving marriage. You can't talk once with your kids and build a lifelong relationship. You have to allow it to be part of your identity; something that is fun to do.

This is different from the "intensity and repetition" school of thought we discussed earlier because you aren't just hammering on your subconscious mind over and over again to try to get rid of your fear of public speaking or give you a million dollars.

I'm talking about creating a lifestyle and personal culture of identifying what is going on and shifting it so that life gets better and better all the time.

Sometimes we resist doing that, usually due to our allergies and addictions. We think that it has to be hard or complicated or that it has to be really emotionally draining or energy consuming. Well, guess what? All those are just interpretations, definitions and frequencies. You can change those. You can make transforming your life something that is fun, exciting, easy, and that works. It can become something that you look forward to.

My wife and I have a routine we do once a week to keep ourselves on track. I want to share it with you, not so you can copy it exactly - your life and family circumstances are different than mine - but so it can spark ideas about what you could be doing to keep thriving.

We start with the kids, doing what we call a "mentor meeting." The goal is to create a fun, engaging time with my wife and I with just one of our children so they feel safe, heard, and ready to transform. Does it always work out that way? Not all the time, but we get close and we're consistent.

First, we pray and set the intention that it's going to be a really great time to talk. They share stories with us. As of the writing of this book, all my children are under the age of 6, so sometimes the stories are hilarious, (but we try not to laugh unless they want us to.) Because they are still small, we let them pick a game they want to play, and while we play, we praise them for all they've done well during the past week.

If you are doing this process, either alone or with family members, it is important to give praise and acknowledgement to your loved ones as well as yourself. Unless you see how far you've come, it's very difficult to know what you can improve. Before I implemented this with myself, I would go in circles. I wouldn't know how I'm progressing. It was difficult to see if my marriage was getting better or worse. It was the same with my relationship with myself, with God, and with my business. An important purpose of these weekly check-ins is to measure your progress. As you learn and use the Alignment process, it is important to do it with purpose, which means you have somewhere you're going. Without this, you'll form negative interpretations and definitions around what you do.

Another example of why this is so important, was when I used to work in the clinic with people who had a stroke and had lost movement in their limbs. Early in my practice, I helped these people with techniques and therapies to help them get back their movement. Back then, it was a lot of repetition and doing different movements and physical techniques over and over. Strangely, I found that no matter how much progress they made, there always came a point when they wanted to give up because they felt like they weren't getting anywhere and hadn't changed at all. I started filming their range of motion during each appointment. Then when they got discouraged, I would show them how much they had actually improved. They had gained an extra 30 degrees of motion in just a couple of weeks, but because they were stuck in a new area, they forgot how far they'd come. The video recording gave them permission to say "Maybe I'm doing better than I thought I was" and keep making progress.

Unless our mind recognizes transformation when it happens, it likes to drag our body backwards to reinforce our former comfort zone. High achievers often suffer the same phenomenon. Without a weekly checkup to acknowledge our achievements, we can easily negate our progress and form an unhelpful definition that "nothing works."

I encourage you to applaud your own changes and remember those gains. Remember the wins. Remember the exciting shifts that happen. And as you remember them, use them as encouraging evidence to get unstuck or counter some allergic or addicted response that might seem difficult to change. Give yourself that evidence to say, "I can change it. It's easy to do. I've done it before."

After we give our kids praise and play a game with them, we talk about the coming week - what we'll be doing - goals and expectations, things that they have to look forward to. This is also a great opportunity for us to see what they want and if there is any way we can help them. We want the whole experience to be fun and exciting, so they are excited for the week. We talk about what they'll be learning, what they'll be doing in school, some of the chores they will complete and projects they will be working on.

Then we address some of the skills or some of the push and pull reactions going on with them that they want help with. For example, during one mentor meeting we talked about how my daughter had some fears about going down an enclosed slide while we were at a park that week. She had stood at the top of the slide and flipped out, had a total meltdown, freaking out that she didn't want to go down the dark slide. Not a super big deal, but when we talked about it during the meeting, she said that she wanted to be able to go down the slide like her sister, and we as parents, wanted to avoid more playground drama.

In my mind I know that this is just an allergy or addiction that she can change pretty easily, and mentor meetings are a great place to address this stuff when she is not reacting in the intensity of the moment. That Sunday, during our mentor meeting, we reflected on it. I said, "Hey, I noticed that when you wanted to go down the slide, you were freaking out and you were scared of the dark. That is something you can change if you'd like to. Do you want to stop having fear around the dark so you can go down the slide?" Then I related to her and told her a story about how I used to be afraid of the dark, so she felt understood and would be willing to open up and want to change for herself. She agreed and said it would be really cool if it was possible.

We did the process, starting with redefining, and then an intuitive alignment which I will share with you later in this book. She had a lot of interpretations of darkness, that it was scary, that there were dark monsters, that she didn't know if she was going to be able to get out. She had all these things that she'd created in her mind and body. Then we did the alignment process and within five or six minutes, that fear went away. That night, she turned off her closet light in her room and slept in the complete dark, a first for her. When we went back to the playground, she had no problem with any of the slides, even the dark ones. She came to me and said, "Dad, I'm not scared of the dark anymore!" Which is super cool. Right?

I love doing alignments with kids, because they are super quick to change. Although she would probably grow out of a fear of the dark eventually, we've helped her and our other children with bigger challenges that might develop into lifelong allergies and addictions if not addressed. For instance, this same daughter had a traumatic experience with a boy when she was in preschool, and it was creating such a big challenge that she wouldn't go to church or dance classes if there was a boy there. She would just sit outside and cry and shake. That Sunday during our mentor meeting, we did the Alignment process with her for 15 minutes. The next day she came to me all excited and said "Dad, I made a new friend today! And he's a boy!" What could have been a big challenge for her was quickly shifted in 15 minutes of alignment.

After we do an alignment with the kids, we wrap up with a prayer and a treat, and they love it. They look forward to it every week, and ask us all day Sunday when it is their turn for a mentor meeting.

Once we are done with the kids, my wife and I have our own weekly check-in. We talk about what went well during the week. We talk about how I saw good in her and the things that she did well that I really appreciated. She shares the same with me. Then we go into discussing our focus for the coming week: What do we need? What are we really working toward? How can we support each other better? Sometimes it's taking care of the kids to give some free time. Sometimes it is supporting more in a certain area of our business. These meetings are a great time for us to test for friction and see what we need to align so we get better results in everything we are working towards. The goal is to help each other as a couple feel like we're one in purpose and we're moving and progressing and our focus is solid.

Whether you have a partner or not, the principles are

1. Reflect on the past and acknowledge your progress;
2. Plan for the future and get focused; and
3. Align to your goals or anything that you struggled with or foresee being an obstacle.

If you do that every week, watch out, you might be shocked by how fast you are able to change. Having these check-ins shows you the progress that you're making and you can look back and say, "Wow, look how far I've come!"

How much further could you be in your marriage or relationship with your kids or in your business, or with your health, if you made one change every week, and it stuck? Imagine the progress you could make.

Most people try to change by focusing on one thing, and it takes them 90 days or 120 days or more. But through the power of aligning, it is possible to shift within hours and continue that momentum by changing many things in the same amount of time. You can build on your progress and look back and see yourself as a completely different individual, more empowered, more focused, more present, more, kind, more loving, more prosperous, more thriving in all areas of your life.

If you're thinking, "I'm already so busy living my life, I don't have time to spend aligning all the time. Will it really make any difference?", you're probably on the verge of a large breakthrough.

Those are the very resistances you need to align, which will get you the fastest possible result. They come because of an addiction to things having to be hard and take a long time. Most of the people I talk to are successful entrepreneurs or have multi-six-figure careers, so of course they're busy. They didn't get where they are without being busy, but the game isn't to be busy, it's to be as productive as possible.

To be as productive as possible, we have to stop. We have to analyze, we have to focus, change our allergies and addictions, tune in and level up. And when you do that, you come with more presence, more energy and more passion, and it makes everything work better.

Imagine you are driving a race car. You intend to win at all costs. Because you're going so fast, you don't have the time to stop and pull over and refuel. So you just keep the pedal on the gas and you're flying. Then one of the wheels starts to bob and weave, but because you're a positive thinker and you don't allow negativity into your life, you keep going and you ignore it. You shove it, you stuff it, you ignore it through working even harder. Then the tire explodes. Because you're a positive thinker and you don't have the time to stop and handle it, you keep going. Then another tire explodes, and another, until all tires are popped and you're going nowhere, and you feel burnt out. Burnout is an indicator that you have not taken the time to align. Whenever you experience overwhelm or burnout, remember to redefine and align. Take the time. It will be worth it.

I know this seems obvious right now, but I'm sharing it so that when that feeling of resistance toward aligning comes up - and I promise it will - you are prepared. Your mind and body are going to fight against it. They're going to make up excuses, and reasons why you shouldn't do it. You are going to be tempted to procrastinate, or to look for the next shiny object to drag you away from making the change you need to make to actually get the result you want.

All this resistance, though, is just patterns, frequencies, allergies and addictions. You can change them. You don't have to be stuck with them any longer. So the game is to just align. If in doubt, align, align, align. It will make everything easier, no matter how long it takes. Even if it took you 10 hours to do an alignment (which it won't) it is still worth it, because everything you do after that 10 hours will be dramatically more effective. You'll end up saving yourself hundreds of hours in the long run. If you take that time to align, you will see a drastic increase in your productivity. If two hours of aligning could save you 20 hours of going in circles, would it be worth it? Of course it would!

I'll share another illustration of how easy this is to implement, and how tempting it is to skip. One day my wife and I were walking around the store together, shopping for one of the kid's birthday parties or something. She began to have some intense pain in her hip. It was getting to a point where it was really bothering her and distracting from what we were trying to accomplish. I suggested that she do a quick intuitive alignment on it.

Now, my wife knows the power of alignment. This whole thing started to help her, after all. But at this moment, walking around the store, she was super resistant to it. She was like "It's probably not going to work right now. I just don't want to do it. It's going to look weird. You have to tap and breathe and smile. I don't want to embarrass myself in public."

So she kept walking around, and her hip pain got worse. Finally she gave in and we did a quick intuitive alignment, right there in the middle of the store. Within five or six minutes, the hip pain completely went away. She regained her ability to walk. She looked at me and she said, "Wow. Sometimes I forget how powerful aligning is!" I laughed and said "I know. We all do." In the moment, we tend to forget, because that is when the resistance kicks in. And the more resistance you have, the more fixing it will probably get you an incredible result.

Remember that after you learn this process and you're resisting it, just tune in and tell yourself "It'll be worth it. Just do it. The more resistance, the better."

By doing what I'm sharing in this book, learning about the power of your body, taking action by redefining and aligning, you'll be able to finally have unshakeable confidence and get the results you actually deserve from all your hard work. Everything you do will become unstoppable. You'll feel fully alive and able to create what you wanted faster than you thought possible.

You'll never have to deal with wondering "How do I change this?" or "What is the solution?" or the feeling that you're not living up to your full potential ever again. I know that's a bold statement, but if you are fully aligned, the only reason you would feel those things is if you had an allergy or an addiction to them. That's the power of alignment. The only thing that's keeping you from what you want is that thought or feeling that counters it. If you align that, then it's gone, and you can finally embrace it through choice.

A final example I want to share here is one of my clients named Yana. She is an amazing coach. She teaches the deeper meaning and symbolism of the Hebrew language, and some really powerful principles. I have learned some really cool things from her about Hebrew and the power of words.

Yana is also a speaker, but she had been doing most of her work for free. One week after our first session together, where I taught her some selling skills and then aligned her so the skills became easy, she was able to make her first $10,000 in a weekend, from an event where she would usually not make anything. And then, from that event, she booked herself solid with speaking engagements for the next several months. It doesn't have to take you years to see a result. When you align, it could take days or even hours. Apply the skills and see the transformation.

Chapter 11:

"The Ten Things You Need to Know to Move at Lightning Speed...and What The Doctors Couldn't Believe"

In this chapter, I want to make sure you have clarity on concepts and actions needed to get the biggest and best results from everything we've covered so far in this book. Then when I teach you the initial Abundance Alignment process you will be off and running.

Here are the ten things to know to really get ready for the biggest transformation possible:

1. Everything is energy. Einstein's famous equation $E=mc^2$ helps us understand that matter and energy are essentially the same, only moving at different speeds. Therefore, by changing the "energy" of something, we can actually change the "mass" or thing itself. Expanding the idea to include metaphysical, as well as quantum and Newtonian physical phenomena, virtually everything is a manifestation of some type of energy. By everything, we mean everything. Your book, the marker board, your left toe, a cell in your body, your eyeball, money, and time. Everything has an "existence": a concept, a thought, an emotion, a perception, a vibration (measurable as a frequency). At the end of the day, that is energy. This is important to know because it will help you wrap your mind around how quickly we are able to shift reactions and results with the Alignment process.

2. Energy, the "stuff" that makes up everything around us, can't be created nor destroyed, but it can be changed or transferred. As you truly grasp this concept, you begin to understand how your current "reality" is not locked. You can truly create a whole new world for yourself. Everything is a summation of different frequencies and energies. Even that "incurable" disease, or bankruptcy, or divorce, or a struggling relationship, or a failed business deal. Frequencies and energies can be changed, thus producing new, more enabling actual realities, which serve you better.

3. Human beings have the ability to transfer energy. We do it all the time by changing hate to love, or love to hate. We transfer energy from fear to courage. Our choices can create health or sickness. If we can do these things, we can also impress our intentions on the physical world around us, because ultimately they are all composed of energy.

4. Our physical bodies, not just our minds, interact with the energy around us and ultimately create the results we achieve in every area of life. Each organ, gland, cell, and energy center of the body has its own response to and influence on what we experience every day. Therefore, attempting to change our lives by only changing the "mind" limits a huge portion of our power, and although it can be done, it takes far longer than shifting or including the body.

5. Responses to everything we experience are interpreted and "stored" very simply as allergies, addictions, or alignment in the body. There is either push and/or pull, or there is peace. If you have something that is working for you, that you want, and nothing else is being sacrificed, that is a state of peace or alignment. If you want something that you don't have, and it is constantly being pushed out of reach, that is an allergy. If you constantly

have something you don't want going on that you can't seem to change, that is an addiction.

6. Being out of alignment constantly puts you in a state of stress that makes life harder, both physically and emotionally. The results you achieve are far smaller than the amount of work you put in, because a large portion of your effort is going toward fighting your allergies and addictions.

7. Allergies, addictions, and alignment are communicated to our minds via definitions. Although physical responses may seem simple, our minds and bodies understand them in the language of neurons, senses, and chemical signals, which include words, images, sounds, emotions, sensations, memories, and experiences. All of these work together to make up our "definitions." Even though the dictionary definition of "love" might be a feeling of affection and connection, the way that it is interpreted by each organ and gland in your body will be different based on the words, images, sounds, emotions, etc. that you've experienced in connection with the word "love."

8. Our definitions are responsible for what we experience and the results we achieve. Every moment of every day these programs are running in every organ and cell in our body, affecting our likes and dislikes, our relationships, our income, our health, all of it. Allergies and addictions cause almost all of the things we don't like about our lives because they are based on compulsions rather than choices.

9. The fastest way to change these allergies and addictions is to align. A state of alignment means being at peace, where the fight and flight responses are neutralized, and you can actually change and choose what type of frequency or energy is in your body. Alignment isn't a magical cure,

instead it simply opens the doorway for you to actually get the results you deserve from your effort, without being stopped or blocked. When someone has an allergy or addiction, they feel like whatever situation they are in is difficult or impossible to change. They've accepted defeat in that area of their life. It feels like they have no choice in the matter because their organs, glands, cells, people, or situations around them are choosing for them. On the flip side, when someone is in full 100% alignment, they are consciously choosing how each organ, gland, and cell responds, and thereby they can change the situation as fast as possible. Alignment is choice, and that is the ultimate place of power.

10. To obtain anything you want in life, simply optimize the Unstoppable Equation.

$$U = S(W+F)/AA$$

- Find the Skills you need,
- Take Action with Focus, and
- Eliminate Allergies and Addictions.

Now, if you can really understand this, then you can feel and change anything you want at lightning speed. You'll have the power of creation inside of you and never be stuck. You'll know you're getting the result as fast as possible. You'll be super confident in yourself and how you treat others and thrive in every area of your life.

You'll also be able to create a ripple effect in your life. You'll see changes in your business, your family, your relationships, your health, your kids, your spouse, your clients, and who you work with. You'll be able to go as far as you desire.

My client Rakesh is a great example of this. Rakesh is a brilliant engineer and programmer and a dedicated father and husband.

He was already very successful in his career and relationships, but he hired me to personally work with him because he knew that there was a deeper level of power and success that he was capable of and wanted to tap into. He also wanted to help his wife, who had a severe disease that was supposedly incurable.

He learned the full Abundance Alignment Technique and took it to heart. He embraced the philosophy and did it consistently. He transformed his lifestyle. After going through multiple alignments, his wife's disease is in remission. The doctors couldn't believe it, and they are now studying her case to see how such a rapid transformation is possible. Rakesh also found his dream job that he loves and pays far more than he could have imagined before learning the Abundance Alignment Technique. He is living in a state of being where he feels like he is fully happy and free and can handle any situation that comes his way with power and confidence.

One more personal story. A couple of years after I developed the Alignment process, I ran a group to certify some clients as Abundance Alignment Technique instructors. My younger brother Zed has always been good at helping people and was interested, so I put him in the group.

Later, he told me that he had been in a really dark place at that time. Although he hadn't told anyone, he'd been dealing with depression and had actually set a date for suicide if nothing changed in his life.

As he went through the group and learned to align, how to speak, and how to sell and market, his perspective gradually began to change. He did an alignment on vaping, something he'd tried and failed to quit many times before.

He said that as soon as he was done, the desire to vape completely went away, and he was able to quit cold turkey. He started to focus on his life mission and helping others instead of being stuck in his own challenges. He got out of depression and suicidal thoughts. Now he has become certified and is teaching other people to transform their own lives as well, and many of his students are having even bigger transformations. I'll always be grateful for what this process did to help my brother Zed. I can't wait to see what it can do for you.

Are you ready?

In the next chapter, I will teach you the basic Alignment process.

Chapter 12:

"Step-by-step Instructions On How to Program Every Cell in Your Body and Get Your Goals in Days Instead of Years"

This chapter has step-by-step instructions on how to do the basic form of Abundance Alignment.

It will get you going and starting to shift.

But first, I want to ask you a question. Would you rather get FANTASTIC results doing something that may seem a little weird, or middle-to-no results doing something that is within your comfort zone?

If you've made it this far, you know we're all about the world of transformation and doing whatever it takes to get results.

The alignment process consists of a few key parts. One is breath patterns. We're going to use breath a lot. We're also going to smile. We're going to breathe in through the nose and out through the mouth and pant like a dog. It's going to seem goofy. You're going to tap on your forehead and do all sorts of weird stuff, but that's okay. I'd rather do weird things and get phenomenal results than do normal things and get horrible ones.

Why does it work? It is similar to what happens when you drop a rock into a lake. The rock represents the allergy or addiction. The allergy or addiction is sending off a ripple of frequency, a wave of something that is either pushing or pulling. It's either attracting what you don't want, or pushing away what you do want.

Physically tapping different parts of your body is in essence like dropping lots of pebbles around that big ripple and nullifying it. So it literally stops those fight/flight responses, those inhibitory push and pulls, those allergies and addictions.

The breathing pattern for the basic alignment consists of in through the nose out through the mouth (in the full Abundance Alignment process, we teach you other breathing patterns for even more powerful effects). This helps calm the body and balance the parasympathetic and sympathetic nervous system so that instead of running or turning on the fight/flight responses, your body relaxes, and you can be fully conscious and receptive. The breath work taps into different states in the brain, as well as hyper oxygenates the body so that undesirable interpretations in your body can be moved and changed.

Smiling is important because when you smile, it fundamentally resets your thinking and feeling, and boosts you to a higher level with an endorphin release. It helps you change your state over and over regardless of what you are working on. It is anchoring positive change - meaning reinforcing the process.

The full Abundance Alignment Technique, which was used by most of the people whose stories I've shared in this book, goes into over 400 different focus areas. It guides you through each organ, gland, chakra, and energy center in the body, as well as "modes" or levels for each one, plus dozens of what I call "inhibitors" and "enablers" so that by the time you are done every single part of you - physically, emotionally, energetically, mentally, everything - is aligned with the thing you want. There is no need to chase limiting beliefs or root causes because we have simply eliminated them all via the process of addressing allergies and addictions on every level and directed every cell in your body to be on the same frequency in regards to the desired outcome. Then, we show you how to "anchor" your alignment, so that if anything ever happens to throw you off, you can instantly return your body to alignment. This is why many of our clients have a complete transformation after one session and never have to do it again on that particular issue.

To cover the full Abundance Alignment Technique is beyond the scope of this book, but you can learn it here: Alignmenteffectbook.com

The entire technique, however, is shaped on the building blocks of the simple alignment I'm about to show you. This process is what allows you to "align" each part of your body.

One lady I know had an intense addiction to eating chips that she couldn't seem to kick. After doing just the process I'm about to show you, she got to the point where she had no desire to eat chips at all.

Description Of Alignment Process

ALIGNMENT:

This process is the part you will repeat often, as needed because it shifts the fight/flight responses. It consists of tapping, breathing, and smiling:

A: Tapping

When doing it on self, start at the top of the forehead and tap up over the top of the head and continue to the rear, down to the base of the neck (C7). This is considered one cycle of tapping. When doing it on someone else, start at the rear base of the neck (C7) and tap down the spine to the beginning of the Lumbar (bottom of rib cage above lower back), also considered one cycle of tapping. The number of taps per cycle isn't important just as long as you tap all the way.

B: Breathing

Breathe in through the nose doing one cycle of tapping. Breathe out through the mouth while doing one cycle of tapping.

Repeat the breathing in and out 3 times for a total of 6 cycles of tapping.

Pant like a dog while doing 3 cycles of tapping.

The entire process is 9 cycles of tapping, 6 breathing in and out, 3 panting.

C: Smile

Simply smile after doing the above process and that completes the aligning portion of the Intuitive Alignment Process.

That's it! You have done your first steps toward alignment. Congrats. Now as simple as this is, this does take practice. The more you practice and master the art of aligning, the more productive you will be.

To see this in action, go to Alignmenteffectbook.com

This technique is very forgiving. There's a lot of variations. Try it, test it out, and get some of the basics down. Then if you're wanting more advanced, more thorough techniques, which were used by the people in most of the stories I shared, then there are resources that you can access and explore. More about those later.

Right now, let's practice.

Find a physical piece of paper, something to write with, and a quiet place, and let's go.

First, write down something important to you that you want to create right now. It could be a better relationship, a new vehicle, $30,000 per month, whatever.

Second, list all the emotions, circumstances, resources, people etc. that stand in your way or are preventing you from achieving your objective. Be specific. Rate the level of obstacle or resistance for each item using a scale of 1-10, with 10 being tons of resistance and it feels impossible, and 1 being no resistance at all.

Next, redefine like we learned in Chapter 6. Write down the old definitions surrounding each thing that is not serving you. Then write down how you want it to be defined. If you are aligning to a phrase, you may need to redefine each word individually.

Then, while doing the aligning process described above, look at each important new definition.

After processing an obstacle, re-rate it. Did your number go up, down, or stay the same?

Many people see their number go down, even after just one alignment. If yours doesn't, don't worry. You probably just have other layers.

Keep going until you've processed every item in your obstacle list.

Now, get in tune with yourself physically. Where in your body do you still feel resistance to the objective? Resistance is usually identified as pain or tightness. It could be in your back, your neck, your forehead, your abdomen, or anywhere else. Tap that place 3-5 times.

Then repeat the aligning process again, focusing your intention on the body part where you had physical resistance manifested.

Re-rate again.

For some people, especially children, doing this a few times is enough to see things shift. When I work on my daughters, I just help them tap where they feel resistance in their body, and pretty soon their body gets into alignment, and they are able to happily go on their way and it's done.

If you don't see massive shifts, that's okay. Maybe you need to do a full alignment on it, but I highly encourage you to keep practicing. The more you do it, the better you'll get at it. Again, remember if you have resistance, just align. Resistance is a frequency that can change and so is the lack of results. Set the target, aim, align, then shoot.

Anything can be solved and shifted. My client Lorraine is a great example of this. Before she decided to join my one-on-one program, she had been trying for years to step into more of her power, and kept getting stuck. When she learned the full process she had a lot of resistance at first. She didn't know how to trust herself and her intuition and tune in. She had issues around spirituality and around feeling like she was capable and good enough. After working with me for only three or four weeks, she said she had completely transformed in every area she'd been looking for. She thought some things would take 20 years to change, but it happened in mere days.

Then we went to the next level. I invited her to think about sharing with other people and her mission on the planet. She realized her goal was not just to feel good about herself, which is great, but maybe she could also coach someone or go serve someone with all the knowledge that she was gaining. She decided to create her own program and go out and share it. I helped her put her program together, come up with her stories, and package it. These are the "skills" that she needed to achieve her dreams. Then the real resistance came up around talking to people and selling something that she had created. That's when it becomes the most fun and the biggest shifts start happening - when you have something inside of you that you want to share but don't know yet how to get it out into the world. Aligning is always the most effective way to clear obstacles once you commit and start moving toward your dream.

Once she answered the questions of "How do I package, find clients, and share in a way that makes sense?" and "How do I feel good enough and have the right balance of skills and aligning so I'm ready to make the biggest difference?" Lorraine turned into a rock star. She is continuing her journey, transforming herself, and doing multiple courses while sharing her message with those she serves

No matter where you are right now, remember to align with purpose. You'll see amazing things come into your life.

SECTION 3:

TAKING IT TO THE NEXT LEVEL AND CREATING TRANSFORMATION THAT LASTS

Chapter 13:

"Every Part of You Will Resist... Change This and You Will Always Thrive"

I hope this doesn't happen to you, but I share it just in case you get stuck again after learning how to align.

You'll try it. You'll do an alignment, maybe just the basic one shared in this book, or maybe you'll decide to dive in and learn the full Abundance Alignment Technique to take your success to the next level. You'll see phenomenal results... but then you'll stop doing it.

I don't know why, but sometimes this happens. The alignment result that was literally a "miracle" before, somehow becomes normal to you. You forget what got you there. It'll feel like you got one awesome outcome, now you don't need to do it anymore.

For instance, I had a client whose son had a traumatic brain injury. She learned the alignment process and did it with her son. She called me back with tears in her eyes and said that he was a completely different person. He was paying attention, respecting her and her husband, actually connecting with people on a whole new level. This was a miracle she had been seeking for years. None of the doctors or other processes she'd used had even come close. She got so excited that she used the process again on herself for weight loss. She hadn't been able to lose pounds for years, no matter how hard she tried. Again, she had awesome results, releasing 8 pounds in a couple of weeks. She had first-hand experience with the power of alignment.

Then she finished her program and we lost touch for a couple of years, and the next thing I know she's posting on Facebook, asking "Does anyone know a solution for _____?" a different thing that could have been easily solved with Abundance Alignment. Come to find out, after the first two "miracles," she thought she'd gotten her value and then forgot to align again! Actually, the "forgetting" was probably actually an allergy to having consistent success long-term - which is something she could align!

So, keep going. Don't stop.

On the other hand, there is an occasional person who will learn about the power of alignment and get super excited, but won't see results immediately. So they quit. Usually right at the point where they were about to have their biggest breakthrough.

If, by chance, this happens to you, look inside and ask "What else needs to be aligned?"

Ask if the thing you are trying to change is a Godly burden. If it is, and you align to it. then you'll feel better about it and you'll learn to see it as an opportunity. You won't accept it as a failure. You will accept it, love it, embrace it, and transform it. If it's still there, and it's a Godly burden, it'll empower you, not disable you. If it's a self-imposed burden, then you'll get rid of it. You'll change it. If you don't change it the first time doing your basic alignment, you'll be persistent. You won't quit. You won't give up until it's changed.

Sometimes what you're going through probably took you decades to create. So you might spend a little bit longer than an hour or two to change it. If it doesn't work the first time; practice, practice, practice.

You might also need help on what phrases or redefinitions to use. I do a live coaching session twice a month to help my clients pinpoint exactly what words to use in their alignments. You might want to learn the full technique, so you can actually be 100% aligned. There are resources that you can tap into to get help, which I've shared throughout this book.

Once I was struggling to get my YouTube ads to be profitable and the agency I'd hired was doing lots of tests, but things seemed to be stagnant. After several weeks, I remembered to use my own process, and did an alignment on my ads.

The phrase I used was something like "My ads convert and make a 10 times return on ad spend." Immediately after aligning, I had this urge to make one tweak to my funnel. Just one tweak. Literally within 24 hours my results spiked. Our entire sales calendar for the next week was filled in a day, and it started to be 10 to 20 times more profitable than before.

Then, I fell into the trap. Seven or eight months down the road, I was having issues with ads again. Something was happening. I thought "Well, I already aligned for my ads. I don't really want to do a full alignment." I justified not doing another alignment to myself and said "I'll just buckle through. I'll just nail it out. It's got to be some messaging. I can figure it out intellectually." And I kept resisting.

Finally, I remembered that resistance is an indicator to start aligning, so I did it again. This time I changed another phrase. Again, within 48 hours, things started to happen. My Facebook ads started to work. I thought to myself, no matter how many times I do this, there are still times when I avoid doing it. I rationalize, and think that I'll just push through it, work harder, work smarter. If I just align every single time, it always makes a difference. It makes everything a lot easier.

The golden rule to avoid more horrible things happening, is that if something's off, it means something's actually off. It means that there is a frequency that is not aligned, that you should probably align first before continuing. Just get yourself to do it.

Think about it like a stair-step. When you align something and step up to the next level, new obstacles will come.

If I align to making $10,000 in a month (or whatever, $10,000 in a week, a day, an hour... whatever bracket you're at. There's always the next level, right?)

Say I aligned the $10,000 in a month. Then all of a sudden, a new obstacle comes in my way or things stop working. Let's say your ads stop working. Or they stopped converting. Or someone quits, or what you are selling has to be redone.

That's actually a good sign.

If you were making $5,000 a month using one set of philosophies and strategies, sometimes the old things stop working so the new things can happen. Sometimes you will see things break down in order to build up. You can't hold on to everything right now and expect to get better results. You have to let go of the non-optimal when they shift.

One of the alignments you might do is "I am safe and feel good letting go of my past progress to allow faster, more effective progress into my life."

Or you could align to "I trust in this process. I trust in myself and in this process and know that I will get even better results as I continue with consistency and focus."

Or, "When I feel reluctance to align, I know I'm about to achieve a new level when I do it anyway. I'm excited to see my new, magnified results as I align"

As you align to one thing, the next thing will be presented that you can align.

So you might align to $10,000 a month, but then the next challenge is "I'm really resisting talking to clients." Cool. That's an alignment: "I love talking to my ideal clients that convert consistently." Boom. Align to that.

Then the next problem might come up. "I feel like I'm over-giving or spending way too much time facilitating." Cool. Now align that.

As you align, you're aligning with purpose, you're progressing, but new things will come into your life that you can then align. You'll always be aligning with purpose and progressing.

There was a guy in one of my programs once who didn't quite understand this principle. Instead of addressing each new thing as it came up, he did the same alignment on the same thing over and over and over every single day.

After a month of doing it, he's like, "Hey, I'm not seeing any results." I asked him, "Well, why are you aligning to the same thing? You have to align with purpose and progression. You aligned to one thing, see what resistance comes up, align to the next thing, see what resistance comes up then. It becomes a game. It becomes a journey where as you implement your weekly check-ins, then you can look back on yourself and say, oh, this is how far I've come. These are the results I've created or achieved. Great. Now I can take my life to the next level and implement and progress faster and even more consistently"

I mentioned my client Rakesh earlier. When he was looking for his ideal job, he was doing interviews and was passionate and focused. He had aligned and he just knew it was going to happen. However, the first job he thought was ideal fell through. I told him, "If you're still aligned, you're not going to have any doubts. If you're really aligned, and that job didn't accept you, then it's not ideal for you, and there is something else that's better for you." So he maintained it. He aligned to the fear of being more bold, more demanding. Then a new opportunity came, and it was even better than the first one, and he got the job. He didn't give up. He didn't quit, because when you're in a state of alignment, you don't quit. You don't stop. You keep going. Whatever you're working on, don't quit. Don't give up, keep going, keep aligning and get any help or coaching that you need. Don't stop. It is worth it.

Chapter 14:

"She Couldn't Take a Shower Or Go To Restaurants Until She Did This…And The Choices You Could Make Right Now to Make or Break Your Own Records"

A great benefit after you start Aligning is that you'll start thinking bigger about what you actually want and could achieve in your life. You'll feel more capable. You'll be a better overall person and create more than you thought was possible.

You'll also start seeing people differently. You'll stop taking offense because offense only happens because of differing definitions; just one definition that counters another person's definition. You will stop and eliminate offense completely. You'll become more likable.

I'm so excited for you to go on this journey of transformation and alignment, because as you dedicate your life and align, you will leave a legacy behind for those who walk a similar path. You can turn around and share the wisdom, wealth, and knowledge with those you care about so that they can progress faster as well.

As you apply these principles, you will start to feel like you're actually doing what you're meant to do. You won't be stopped by limitations anymore. You will be free to live your calling and fulfill your mission. You are creating a conscious world, and this is going to be so amazing. It's going to help you grow your business. It's going to help you be more driven. It's going to help make more income. You're going to come alive in your physical health, and you will be more in tune in with your spirituality. You'll build more powerful relationships.

It will truly change your life if you choose it to, because at the end of the day, it's your choice. You can choose not to align. That's your choice. You can choose to run around in circles. That's your choice. You can choose to make this really hard. That's your choice. You could choose to have this not work for you. That's your choice.

Everything is a choice. So much of what we are battling every day are simply frequencies in our bodies allergies and addictions that can be changed. The very thing that you think "has to be," is that way only because you've chosen it to be.

You could choose to believe that you can change. Or, you could choose to believe that it's not your choice and everything is just genetics. You could believe that that's impossible to change.

You can choose to believe that everything I'm saying is a bunch of BS, meaning "belief systems."

You can choose to believe that nothing is going to work for you.

You could choose to believe that everything is going to work for you.

And you could choose to believe it in every part of your body, or just in your mind.

Either way, all of those things are still your choices.

So my question to you is what are you going to choose? Are you going to choose to align? Are you going to choose to thrive? Or are you going to choose to settle, to accept defeat?

It's up to you.

One of my clients, Jessica, had a severe nickel allergy. So severe that if she took a shower, she'd break out due to the nickel in the pipes. She couldn't go around any restaurants because of the nickel in the food. This had been going on for years and years. It affected her business. It affected her relationship. She couldn't kiss her boyfriend after he ate any type of seafood because of the allergy. It was horrible.

These definitions and interpretations were so real to her. She had tried so many different things. However, when she came into my space she was willing to open up to all of the stories and evidence I shared with her. She saw how many people had changed. She knew that if there was a way, this could be it.

So she made the investment and put in the time to learn the full Abundance Alignment Technique. I'm happy to say she has been able to not only eat at restaurants, but take showers without any reaction. She can eat food with nickel in it now without any reactions. More than that, it has empowered and enabled her to see that she doesn't have to accept defeat in any area of her life. She can be a victor and a winner in every part of her life, relationships, health and in her business.

Here's the crazy thing. You might just think. "Cool, I'm not allergic to nickel." But more than that, when you align something, it can change your whole reality. Now her business is also thriving.

Because you are the creator of all of the things in your life, if you improve yourself in one area, all areas improve.

Monica is another amazing client of mine. Monica has done lots of alignments on herself and had phenomenal results. She went through my certification program. She's amazing. She was able to work on one of her relatives that was suffering with a major disease, and after a few months and a few alignments he is now disease free.

(Remember, We aren't doctors and we don't cure, diagnose or treat anything. We can't promise anything. We get life changing testimonials from people. This is just information. :)

Now for you, What situation are you focused on? What's your number one goal? What do you really want to create in your life? Write that thing out. Then map out all the resistances, the reactions, the distractions, the temptations, the fears that you might have around that thing. Next, imagine your life without those things. What if they were just gone? What if they were non-existent? What if it didn't have to be a reality anymore? What if it could be your choice? How would you show up differently? How would you treat yourself differently? How would you treat loved ones differently, your business differently? I hope you're beginning to see the power of alignment.

Chapter 15:

"Three Things That Will Tell You Everything You Need to Know About Yourself"

Before we wrap up, I want to share three things that you can do right now that will get you closer to what you really want.

1. Take note of what you turn to when you're avoiding something. When things go wrong, when you are frustrated, what is your go-to distraction?

This is important because if you can understand what your habits are - the things you turn to out of avoidance - that shows you what you can align. If you pay close enough attention, you will begin to recognize in what areas your body is limiting your ability to create the life of your dreams.

So pay attention. What are you stuck on? What are you avoiding? These are allergies and addictions. Write them down.

2. Look for things that you keep wishing would be different. Notice the things you want to change or that you complain about. These are important because these are hopes and aspirations that you're pushing away. The things that you wish for, that you hope for, that you would want to change deep down inside. Maybe you complain about it, or maybe you stuff it down and don't admit it, but you wish you could change it. Those are the things that you've actually formed allergic responses to.

3. Look at what you wrote down for number one and two. These are stepping stones to help you see what you can actually change. See them as opportunities instead of blocks and problems. They can be alignments and ways to transform your life. Use them as mirrors to show you what is inside of you that needs to change in order to get where you want to go.

One time, I found myself getting really distracted from my work because I wanted to play games. I looked forward to the end of the day and had this drive, this compulsion to play. So I said, "Okay I need to stop doing this." And I stopped. Then emotions and feelings started to well up. They showed me what was actually going on. I wanted something to help me feel like I was making progress. I wanted to feel like I was having fun and in control. It showed me things that I was actually pushing away in my business and family life.

So, I created a phrase to align to, something like "I can progress and have fun," "I'm in control regardless of games," and "I don't need games to feel fulfilled. I can have fun with or without them."

After aligning, I still like to play games, but it's not out of a compulsion or avoiding things in my life. Plus, to me aligning is a game. It's a fun game. It's a game to be explored, to be taken to the next level of progress.

This is another challenge with most ways people try to change. If someone has a smoking addiction they might just cut it out cold turkey and stop, but it doesn't necessarily change the energetic pattern. It might change the habit, but the pattern will pick up somewhere else. I've seen people who stopped smoking cold turkey, but without shifting the underlying allergies and addictions they just turn to something else to fill the void. You probably have seen this too.

In your own life, you may have implemented a lot of things with a lot of work that ended up producing temporary results. Because they didn't address the core issue in the body, where it was actually held, nothing really changed.

I had a client named Lynda who joined a coaching program with a prestigious high-end coach, one that everybody knows. The coach in her group said "Okay, look, we're just going to teach you to do a lot of things. You've just got to push through and do it. We don't go into any life experiences, problems, or issues. My job is just to make sure you do what you need to do."

For Lynda, it turned out to be a horrible investment. It was over $10,000. She didn't get the promised value out of it because the coach shared all the skills and attacked it through the mind, but her body still was aching to be addressed. She wanted to say, "Please help me change completely, in my core." After joining me, she said, it was like a breath of fresh air and the best investment she ever made, simply because we helped her actually change.

I already mentioned the $80,000, 25-35 hour a week program I went through for personal transformation that was primarily focused on the mind. Occasionally the body was involved, but it was treated as an entirely separate thing. They didn't tie the two together. I did this for over a year and still wasn't done, because there was always more. And I thought, "Wow, there has got to be a faster, more effective way where you don't have to spend $60-$75k, or even a hundred thousand dollars to experience a lasting change.

That's why you are here. If you're looking for lasting changes, remember to ALSO address the body, eliminate allergies and addictions, and align.

Chapter 16:

"The Secret Sauce That Allows You to Collapse Time... And What to do Next"

You have the ability to change anything in your life, but you don't have to do it alone.

If you truly want to collapse time, get every cell in your body working with you.

My team and I would love to take you by the hand and help you do this.

With the right team, all the pieces of the Unstoppable Equation work for you, not against you.

The faster you gain the unhindered Skills for your vision, the bigger you will achieve.

The more accountability, Work and Focus you put in, the more you will be able to implement those skills.

And if you eliminate the Allergies and Addictions and truly Align, it will be like adding jet fuel to everything you are doing.

The full Abundance Alignment Technique is amazing. It is very thorough. It is all mapped out, exactly what to do in what order, from "opening the door" so you are ready to change, all the way to "anchoring." We go through body systems, organs, glands, chakras. Then into inhibitors, which cover all the things that stop you from alignment; and enablers, which help you create the highest form of alignment.

The anchoring process is one of the coolest parts. Essentially, it is like you're driving a vehicle and you put on the cruise control. If you push the brake, but then hit refresh on the cruise control, it'll bring you back up to speed.

That's what anchoring does. After you align, you anchor so that you can consistently, reliably, and easily refresh it. If life happens and throws things off, you can bring yourself back to a hundred percent alignment, even if and when toxic situations come your way. It makes things so easy and convenient.

By the time you finish with the Abundance Alignment Technique, it is done. There is nothing left to shift. You've covered everything to put your body in a state of complete alignment.

That's why we see such incredible results.

The system and process is complete, one and done.

I'd love you to experience it.

If you want to learn more, go to Alignmenteffectbook.com

Another way we'd love to support you is for you to join our weekly group alignments. These are super fun, uplifting and powerful experiences where we go through multiple variations of the alignment on pressing issues with an amazing group of powerful people. We also have a list of dozens and dozens of guided alignments on different topics that you can go through on demand. If you're struggling with something specific, instead of having to come up with it yourself, or figure out the next step, you can watch a group alignment and experience the shift, and then you are done. There are tens of thousands of dollars of value in all the alignments that we've done, and you can have them all at your fingertips. I have pages of testimonials and experiences of people who've been through them.

So again, if you would like to explore what the full alignment process looks like and how to access it, you can go to Alignmenteffectbook.com

I suggest you do this, because even though you can get quite a bit out of a book, high achievers want to get to the source and implement with full effectiveness now. You want to get there quickly. You could take the basic alignment principles I've given you and probably see some results. Personally, using the full process to fully clear even one allergy or addiction is literally worth tens of thousands, potentially millions of dollars because once I clear myself up, everything else works -. including my health and my relationships with my wife and kids, which is far more valuable than anything in business.

Alignment is a physical, full body experience. Reading this book is awesome but reading alone is more of a mental experience. I want you to have the full effect, to apply it in both your mind and your body and to live it. I'd love to guide you via interactive examples so that you can feel the full effect for yourself. Another way to do that is to join my Facebook group at, Tylerfb.com.

In this free group, I have mini trainings and group alignments. I'd love for you to be a part of our community. There are some pretty awesome people to connect with and who will welcome you into the group. We'll also share some other ways to get involved and get your questions answered.

Also, for those who want the highest level of transformation, I occasionally open a few spots to work directly with me. If you are willing to go there, show up as your best self, and become truly unstoppable go to Alignmenteffectbook.com to see if you qualify.

I thank you for taking the time to read this book. I hope to meet you soon in the Abundance Alignment Technique courses and community.

You are magnificent. Lasting change is possible.

See you on the inside.

Let's Align.

To access video demonstrations, case studies, and additional opportunities I've mentioned, be sure to check out Alignmenteffectbook.com

Made in United States
Cleveland, OH
05 September 2025